London

DOVER LANGUAGE GUIDES

# 1001 EASY FRENCH PHRASES

Heather McCoy, Ph.D.

DOVER PUBLICATIONS, INC., Mineola, New York

*Copyright*

Copyright © 2010 by Heather McCoy
All rights reserved.

*Bibliographical Note*

*1001 Easy French Phrases* is a new work, first published by
Dover Publications, Inc., in 2010.

*Library of Congress Cataloging-in-Publication Data*

McCoy, Heather.
  1001 easy French phrases / Heather McCoy.
    p. cm.
  Text in English and French.
  Includes bibliographical references and index.
  ISBN-13: 978-0-486-47620-9
  ISBN-10: 0-486-47620-0
  1. French language—Conversation and phrase books—English.   I. Title.
  II. Title: One thousand and one easy French phrases.
  PC2121M53 2010
  448.3'421—dc22

                                                        2010034729

Manufactured in the United States by Courier Corporation
47620002
www.doverpublications.com

# Table of Contents

# Introduction

This book is designed for the traveler or casual user of French who is looking for a handy and manageable guide to basic French phrases. The phrases included in this convenient volume are some of the basic tools for communication and comprehension that you are likely to need in a variety of French-speaking contexts.

The primary focus of *1001 Easy French Phrases* is daily communication. You will find linguistic structures that focus on describing yourself and others; asking simple questions that one might need when traveling; and interacting in a variety of situations. The phrases have been organized thematically so that you can easily find vocabulary and sentence structures that apply to a specific context. Special attention has been paid to organizing phrases so that you can substitute the vocabulary you need in order to create your own meaning, such as in the following example:

"Je voudrais prendre . . ." *(I'd like to have . . . )*
. . . une bière (a beer)
. . . un café (a coffee)

You will be able to use this book in a variety of ways, either by preparing for a trip by reading a few sections a day, or by using it on-the-spot by flipping to the section that is most pertinent at that moment. Our hope is that you will find the phrases useful and flexible, enabling you to effectively create your own meanings. If you are interested in going beyond the phrases presented in this book, please refer to the Appendix on page 95, which includes verb conjugations, an outline of several key grammatical points, and resources for continued learning.

## French Pronunciation

*1001 Easy French Phrases* uses a phonetic transcription as an aid to correct pronunciation. (See "Scheme of Pronunciation," below.) This transcription is located directly beneath the French entry in the text. Here are some general principles of pronunciation:

## Nasalization

In French, a vowel is nasalized when it is followed by a single *m* or *n* in the same syllable. The transcription of these nasalized vowels appears as:

*-an, -am, -em, -en* -> ahn, ehn
*-in, -im* -> ihn, ihm
*-on, -om* -> ohn, ohm
*-um, -un* -> uhn

To produce a nasalized vowel, quickly pass the air through both the nose and the mouth at the same time. The *m* or *n* isn't pronounced after the nasal vowel, as follows:

*français* -> frahn-say; *temps* -> tahn
*pain* -> pihn; *printemps* -> prihn-tehn
*bon* -> bohn
*quelqu'un* -> kell-kuhn

## Silent Final Consonants

In French, most consonants at the end of a word are silent, although there are exceptions to this rule: *c*, *f*, and *l*. The consonant *r* also is pronounced, but is silent when occurring in the endings *-er* and *-ier*.

## The French r

The French *r* can be one of the most challenging sounds for English speakers to pronounce. Pronunciation of the *r* will depend upon the region of the French-speaking world that you are visiting. In some areas, the French *r* can resemble the Italian or Spanish *r*—produced by rolling it on the tip of the tongue. The Parisian *r* is a more gutteral sound: it's helpful to imagine the sound being produced in the back of the throat, the same place that produces the *h* in "ahoy." The *r* is voiced, meaning that there is a slight vibration of the vocal cords.

### The Plural s

As mentioned above, consonants at the end of words normally are not pronounced. Make special note of this when pronouncing the *s* that denotes the plural:

*Le chat* -> luh-shah
*Les chats* -> lay-shah

Notice how the pronunciation of the noun *chat* does not change between the singular and the plural. This is quite different from English, and is important for English speakers to remember.

### Liaison

A final consonant that is normally silent is pronounced when it comes before a vowel or *h*. This phenomenon is called *liaison*. Note the following change:

A final *s* before a consonant: *des livres* -> day-leev-ruh
A final *s* before a vowel: *des animaux* -> daze-ehn-ee-moh

The rules for liaison can be somewhat complex, so simply pay attention to the phonetic transcriptions in order to get a feel for when its usage is appropriate.

### Stress

The last syllable of a French word is usually stressed:

*Beaucoup* -> boh-<u>koo</u>

However, when the last syllable is an unstressed *e* (*uh* in the transcription used here), the next-to-the-last syllable receives the stress:

*Formidable* -> for-mee-<u>dah</u>-bluh

You will also notice that in addition to the stress at the end of a word, there also is stress at the end of a phrase:
*Je suis américain et travaille au musée d'art contemporain.* -> zhuh swee <u>za</u>-mary-<u>kihn</u> ay tra-vy oh moo-<u>zay</u> <u>dar</u> cohn-<u>tehn</u>-por-<u>ihn</u>.

# Scheme of Pronunciation

| Letters | Transcription | Example | Notes |
|---------|---------------|---------|-------|
| a | a | as in *ask*, but cut short | |
| | ah | as in *father* | |
| ai | ay | as in *play* | |
| | y | as in *why* | |
| au | oh | as in *bow* | See note on *o* below. |
| b | b | as in *bear* | |
| c | k | as in *car* | Pronounced *k* before *a*, *o*, or *u* |
| | s | as in *sun* | Pronounced *s* before *e* and *i* |
| ç | s | as in *sun* | |
| d | d | as in *danger* | Formed by touching tongue tip to teeth |
| e, è | eh | as in *met* | |
| é | ay | as in *play* | |
| e, eu, œu | uh | as in *bubble* | |
| f | f | as in *fan* | |
| g | g | as in *give* | Before *a*, *o*, and *u* |
| g | zh | as in *garage* | Before *e* and *i* |
| gn | ny | as in *canyon* | |
| h | silent | | |
| i | ee | as in *feet* | |
| j | zh | as in *garage* | |
| k | k | as in *kernel* | |

| | | | |
|---|---|---|---|
| l | l | as in *lap* | |
| m | m | as in *me* | |
| n | n | as in *note* | |
| o | oh | as in *toe* | |
| oi | wa | as in *want* | |
| ou | oo | as in *boom* | |
| p | p | as in *pat* | |
| ph | f | as in *fan* | |
| q | k | as in *kernel* | |
| r | r | as in *red* | See section above. |
| s | ss | as in *lass* | At the beginning of the word or when doubled |
| | z | as in *zap* | When between two vowels |
| | silent | | At the end of a word, unless followed by a vowel. See section above. |
| t | t | as in *tip* | |
| th | t | as in *tip* | |
| u | oo | no English equivalent | Formed by saying "ee," moving lips into rounded position without moving tongue. |
| v | v | as in *vote* | |
| w | v, w | as in *vote, win* | |
| x | ks | as in *licks* | |
| y | ee | as in *greet* | |
| z | z | as in *zoo* | |

# 1001
## EASY
# FRENCH
## PHRASES

# Chapter 1
## Greetings and Everyday Expressions

## GREETINGS, INTRODUCTIONS, AND SOCIAL CONVERSATION

One of the ways in which French differs from English is that French uses formal and informal registers of language. These are expressed in the choice of the subject pronoun (*vous* is formal; *tu* is informal); the form of the verb; and, sometimes, in the way a question is formed. Always address adults whom you don't know well using the formal form of the verb, and reserve the informal for friends and children. It is interesting to note that Americans have a tendency to be informal in many situations in which the French prefer to interact formally. We've indicated below whenever a given sentence is formal or informal.

You will discover that although the subject pronoun for "we" is *nous*, the pronoun *on* frequently is used instead. You can usually tell by the context whether the speaker using *on* is referring to someone in general, or to the first-personal plural form "we."

As far as greetings are concerned, keep in mind that these are quite important, and are another way that the formal and informal registers of language are expressed. To show politeness, greet a shopkeeper or hotel employee with *"Bonjour Madame"* or *"Bonjour Monsieur."* And a smile is universal!

You also will note that another difference between French and English is that nouns in French are either masculine or feminine. This has nothing to do with actual gender—say, the inherent masculine nature of *le stylo* (the pen), so it's better to memorize the gender of a noun rather than try to figure out this system of classification! Another important aspect to remember about the gender of nouns in French is that articles, adjectives, pronouns, and some verbs must agree with nouns in gender and number. We have indicated this below where appropriate by providing both the masculine and feminine forms, with the feminine form indicated either with an "e" in parentheses or given in a separate example. Note that when choosing sentences to describe yourself, you'll want to choose the appropriate form.

1.  Good morning.    *Bonjour.*    **Bohn-**<u>zhoor</u>

2.  Good evening.    *Bonsoir.*    **Bohn-**<u>swahr</u>

3.  Good night. (bedtime)    *Bonne nuit.*    **Buhn** <u>nwee</u>

4.  Hello.    *Bonjour.*    **Bohn-**<u>zhoor</u>

5.  Hi.    *Salut.*    <u>**Sah**</u>-loo

6.  Good-bye.    *Au revoir.*    **Oh ruh** <u>vwahr</u>

7.  See you soon.    *À bientôt.*    **Ah** <u>byehn</u>-**toh**

8.  See you tonight!    *À ce soir!*    **Ah suh** <u>swahr</u>

9.  See you tomorrow!    *À demain!*    **Ah duh-**<u>mihn</u>

10.  See you later! (formal)    *À plus tard!*    **Ah** <u>ploo</u> **tar**

11.  See you later! (informal)    *À plus!*    **Ah** <u>ploos</u>

12.  Have a nice day.    *Bonne journée.*    <u>**Buhn**</u> **zhoor-nay**

13.  Have a nice evening.    *Bonne soirée.*    <u>**Buhn**</u> **swa-ray**

14.  My name is . . .    *Je m'appelle* . . .    <u>**Zhuh**</u> **ma-pel**

15.  Allow me to introduce you to . . . (most formal)
     *Permettez-moi de vous présenter* . . .
     **Per-meh-tay mwah** <u>duh</u> **voo** <u>pray</u>-**zehn-tay**

|  | | |
|---|---|---|
| my colleagues. | *mes collègues.* | may koll-<u>eg</u> |
| my friend. (m—masculine) | *mon ami.* | mohn ah-mee |
| my friend. (f—feminine) | *mon amie.* | mohn ah-mee |

16.  This is . . . (formal)    *Je vous présente* . . .
     **Zhuh voo** <u>pray</u>-**zehnt**

|  | | |
|---|---|---|
| my wife. | *ma femme.* | ma fahm |
| my husband. | *mon mari.* | mohn mah-<u>ree</u> |

|  |  |  |
|---|---|---|
| my spouse/partner. | *mon conjoint.* | mohn <u>kon</u>-zhwehn |
| my boyfriend. | *mon copain.* | mohn <u>co</u>-pihn |
| my girlfriend. | *ma copine.* | ma <u>co</u>-peen |

17. This is . . . (informal)  *Voici . . .*   Vwa-<u>see</u>

|  |  |  |
|---|---|---|
| my daughter. | *ma fille.* | ma fee |
| my son. | *mon fils.* | mohn feese |
| my child. | *mon enfant.* | mohn <u>ehn</u>-fehn |
| my children. | *mes enfants.* | maze <u>ehn</u>-fehn |
| my brother. | *mon frère.* | mohn fraire |
| my sister. | *ma sœur.* | ma suhr |
| my family. | *ma famille.* | ma <u>fa</u>-mee |

18. Pleased to meet you.
    *Enchanté. (if you are male)     Enchantée. (if you are female)*
    Ehn-<u>shehn</u>-tay

19. How nice to see you again. (formal)
    *Quel plaisir de vous revoir.*
    Kell play-<u>zeer</u> duh voo ruh-<u>vwahr</u>

20. Nice to see you again. (informal)   *Quel plaisir de te revoir.*
    Kell play-<u>zeer</u> duh tuh ruh-<u>vwahr</u>

21. I am here on a business trip.   *Je suis ici en voyage d'affaires.*
    Zhuh swee <u>zee-see</u> ehn voy-<u>yahzh</u> da-<u>fare</u>

22. We're on vacation.   *On est en vacances.*
    Ohn et ehn <u>va</u>-kanse

23. I work for . . .  *Je travaille pour . . .*   Zhuh tra-vy <u>poor</u>

24. What line of work are you in?   *Quelle est votre profession?*
    Kell ay <u>vote</u> pro-fess-yion

25. Where do you work?   *Où est-ce que vous travaillez?*
    Oo ess-kuh voo tra-vy-<u>yay</u>

26. I am . . .  *Je suis . . .*   <u>Zhuh</u> swee
    . . . a stay-at-home mom.    . . . *femme au foyer.*
    fahm oh-<u>fwa</u>-yay

    . . . a doctor.    . . . *médecin.*   <u>made</u>-sihn

    . . . a teacher.    . . . *prof.*   **prohf**

    . . . a university professor.    . . . *un(e) universitaire.*
**uhn / oon oo-<u>nee</u>-vers-uh-<u>tare</u>**

    . . . a business man.    . . . *homme d'affaires.*   **umm <u>dah</u>-fare**

    . . . a business woman.    . . . *femme d'affaires.*
**fahm <u>dah</u>-fare**

    . . . an architecte.    . . . *architecte.*   **are-<u>shee</u>-tekt**

    . . . an engineer.    . . . *ingénieur.*   **ihn-<u>zhayn</u>-yer**

    . . . a scientist.    . . . *un(e) scientifique.*
**uhn / oon see-<u>yehn</u>-tee-feek**

27. I am retired.   *Je suis à la retraite.*
**Zhuh swee ah la <u>ruh</u>-tret**

28. I am currently unemployed.   *Je suis au chômage.*
**Zhuh swee oh <u>shoh</u>-mazh**

29. I'm a college student.   *Je suis étudiant(e).*
**Zhuh swee zay-too-<u>dyehn</u>**   **Zhuh swee zay-too-<u>dyehnt</u>**

30. I'm studying . . .   *J'étudie . . .*   **Zhay-too-<u>dee</u>**

    . . . English.    . . . *l'anglais.*   **lehn-<u>glay</u>**

    . . . history.    . . . *l'histoire.*   **lee-<u>stwahre</u>**

    . . . French.    . . . *le français.*   **luh frehn-<u>say</u>**

    . . . biology.    . . . *la biologie.*   **la <u>bee-oh</u>-low-zhee**

    . . . chemistry.    . . . *la chimie.*   **la <u>shee</u>-mee**

    . . . engineering.    . . . *l'ingénierie.*   **lihn-<u>zhayn</u>-yoor-ee**

31. I am a friend of Robert's.
*Je suis un ami de Robert. (if you are male)*
*Je suis une amie de Robert. (if you are female)*
**Zhuh swee uhn ahh-mee <u>duh</u> rho-bear**
**Zhuh swee oon ahh-mee <u>duh</u> rho-bear**

32. How are you? (formal)   *Comment allez-vous?*
**<u>Kuh-muh</u> tall-ay voo**

33. How are you? (informal)   *Ça va?*   **Sah <u>vah</u>**

34. Fine, thanks. And you?    *Je vais bien, merci. Et vous? (formal)*
*Je vais bien, merci. Et toi? (informal)*
**Zhuh vay <u>byehn</u> mare-see. Ay voo**
**Zhuh vay <u>byehn</u> mare-see. Ay twah**

35. All right.    *Ça va.*    **Sah <u>vah</u>**

36. Very well.    *Ça va très bien.*    **Sah vah <u>tray</u> byehn**

37. Where are you from? (formal)    *D'où venez-vous?*
**Doo vuh-nay <u>voo</u>**

38. Where are you from? (informal)    *Tu viens d'où?*
**Too vyihn <u>doo</u>**

39. I am from Boston.    *Je suis de Boston.*
**Zhuh swee duh bos-ton**

40. I am American.
*Je suis américain. (m.)    Je suis américaine. (f.)*
**Zhuh swee za-mary-<u>kihn</u>    Zhuh swee za-mary-<u>kenn</u>**

41. Are you French?
*Vous êtes français? (m.)*
*Vous êtes française? (f.)*
**Voo zet frehn-<u>say</u>**
**Voo zet frehn-<u>sez</u>**

42. How is your family?
*Comment va votre famille? (formal)*
*Comment va ta famille? (informal)*
**Kuh-muh vah <u>vote</u> fah-mee    Kuh-muh vah <u>tah</u> fah-mee**

43. How are your friends?
*Comment vont vos amis? (formal and when addressing a group)*
*Comment vont tes amis? (informal)*
**Kuh-muh vohn <u>voze</u> ah-mee    Kuh-muh vah <u>taze</u> ah-mee**

44. Please have a seat. (formal)    *Asseyez-vous.*    **Ah-say-yay <u>voo</u>**

45. Please have a seat. (when addressing a group)    *Asseyez-vous.*
**Ah-say-yay <u>voo</u>**

46. Please have a seat. (informal)    *Assieds-toi.*
**Ah-see-yay <u>twah</u>**

47.   What a pleasure to see you.
      *Quel plaisir de vous voir. (formal and when addressing a group)*
      *Quel plaisir de te voir. (informal)*
      **Kell play-zeer duh voo <u>vwahr</u>     Kell play-zeer duh tuh <u>vwahr</u>**

48.   Pleasure to meet you.
      *Je suis ravi(e) de faire votre connaissance.*
      **Zhuh swee <u>rah</u>-vee duh fare <u>vote</u> con-ay-sance**

49.   What a pleasant dinner.     *Quel dîner agréable.*
      **Kell dee-nay ag-ray-<u>ahb</u>-luh**

50.   Give my regards to your family.
      *Mes amitiés à votre famille. (formal)*
      *Mes amitiés à ta famille. (informal)*
      **Maze ah-mee-tyay ah <u>vote</u> fah-mee**
      **Maze ah-mee-tyay ah <u>tah</u> fah-mee**

51.   Come visit us.     *Venez nous rendre visite.*
      **Vuh-nay noo rand-ruh <u>vee-zeet</u>**

52.   Come back and see us.     *Revenez nous voir.*
      **<u>Ruh</u>-vuh-nay noo vwahr**

53.   We would love to visit you. (formal)
      *On aimerait bien vous rendre visite.*
      **Oh nem-er-ay <u>byehn</u> voo rand-ruh vee-zeet**

54.   Can I visit you sometime? (informal)
      *Je peux te rendre visite un jour?*
      **Zhuh puh tuh rand-ruh <u>vee-zeet</u> uhn zhoor**

55.   May I stop over and see you? (formal and group)
      *Puis-je passer vous voir?*
      **Pwee-zhuh <u>pah-say</u> voo <u>vwahr</u>**

56.   May I stop over and see you? (informal)
      *Je peux passer te voir?*     **Zhuh puh <u>pah-say</u> tuh <u>vwahr</u>**

57.   What is your address?
      *Quelle est votre adresse? (formal)*
      *Quelle est ton adresse? (informal)*
      **Kell ay vote ah-<u>dress</u>     Kell ay tone ah-<u>dress</u>**

58.  What is your phone number?
*Quel est votre numéro de téléphone? (formal)*
*Quel est ton numéro de téléphone? (informal)*
**Kell ay vote noo-mare-<u>oh</u> duh tay-lay-<u>phone</u>**
**Kell ay tone noo-mare-<u>oh</u> duh tay-lay-<u>phone</u>**

59.  What is your email address?
*Quelle est votre adresse courriel? (formal)*
*Quelle est ton adresse courriel? (informal)*
**Kell ay vote ah-<u>dress</u> koo-ree-ehl**
**Kell ay tone ah-<u>dress</u> koo-ree-ehl**

60.  Here is my address.    *Voici mon adresse.*
**Vwa-see mohn ah-<u>dress</u>**

61.  Here is my cell-phone number.
*Voici mon numéro de portable.*
**Vwa-see mohn noo-mare-<u>oh</u> duh por-<u>tahble</u>**

62.  Here is my website address.
*Voici l'adresse de mon site Internet.*
**Vwa-see lah-<u>dress</u> duh mohn seet In-tare-<u>net</u>**

63.  May I see you again?    *Puis-je vous revoir?*
**<u>Pwee</u>-zhuh voo ruh-<u>vwahr</u>**

## MAKING YOURSELF UNDERSTOOD

When approaching a stranger to ask a question, remember to show politeness by starting with "*Excusez-moi, Madame*" when addressing a woman and "*Excusez-moi, Monsieur*" when addressing a man.

64.  Do you speak English?
*Vous parlez anglais? (formal)*
*Tu parles anglais? (informal)*
**Voo pah-lay ehn-<u>glay</u>    Too pahl ehn-<u>glay</u>**

65.  Does anyone here speak English?
*Il y a quelqu'un qui parle anglais ici?*
**Eel ya <u>kell-kuhn</u> kee pahl ehn-glay <u>ee-see</u>**

66.  I speak a little French.    *Je parle un peu français.*
**<u>Zhuh</u> pahl uhn <u>puh</u> frehn-say**

67.  I only speak English.    *Je ne parle que l'anglais.*
     <u>Zhuh</u> nuh pahl <u>kuh</u> lehn-<u>glay</u>

68.  I don't speak French well.    *Je ne parle pas bien français.*
     <u>Zhuh</u> nuh pahl pah <u>byehn</u> frehn-say

69.  Can you translate this word?    *Pouvez-vous traduire ce mot?*
     Poo-vay voo <u>trah</u>-dweer suh <u>moh</u>

70.  What is the English equivalent of this phrase?
     *Quel est l'équivalent de cette phrase en anglais?*
     Kell ay luh-kee-vah-lehn <u>duh</u> set frahz en ehn-<u>glay</u>

71.  I understand.    *Je comprends.*    <u>Zhuh</u> kom-<u>prehn</u>

72.  I don't understand.    *Je ne comprends pas.*
     <u>Zhuh</u> nuh <u>kom-prehn</u> pah

73.  Do you understand?    *Vous comprenez?*    <u>Voo</u> com-pren-<u>ay</u>

74.  Do you understand me?    *Vous me comprenez?*
     <u>Voo</u> muh com-pren-<u>ay</u>

75.  Say it again, please.    *Répétez, s'il vous plaît.*
     Ray-pay-<u>tay</u> see voo <u>play</u>

76.  Please speak more slowly, please.
     *Parlez moins vite, s'il vous plaît.*
     Pah-lay <u>mwehn veet</u> see voo <u>play</u>

77.  Write it down, please.    *Pouvez-vous l'écrire, s'il vous plaît?*
     Poo-vay voo <u>lay-kreer</u> see voo <u>play</u>

78.  What does this mean?    *Que veut dire cela?*
     Kuh vuh deer suh-<u>lah</u>

79.  How do you say "dog" in French?
     *Comment dit-on "dog" en français?*
     Kuh-muh <u>dee-ton</u> dog ehn frehn-<u>say</u>

80.  What does this mean in English?
     *Que veut dire cela en anglais?*
     Kuh vuh deer suh-<u>lah</u> ehn ehn-<u>glay</u>

## USEFUL WORDS AND EXPRESSIONS

81. Yes.  *Oui.*  **Wee**

82. No.  *Non.*  **Noh**

83. Maybe.  *Peut-être.*  **Puh <u>tet</u>-ruh**

84. Please.  *S'il vous plaît. (formal)*  *S'il te plaît. (informal)*
**See voo <u>play</u>**  **Seel tuh <u>play</u>**

85. Thanks (a lot).  *Merci (beaucoup).*  **<u>Mare</u>-see (<u>boh</u>-koo)**

86. Thanks, that's very kind.  *Merci, c'est gentil.*
**<u>Mare</u>-see say zhan-<u>tee</u>**

87. You're welcome. (formal)  *Je vous en prie.*
**Zhuh voo <u>zehn</u> pree**

88. You're welcome. (informal)  *De rien.*  **<u>Duh</u> ree-ehn**

89. Pardon?  *Pardon?*  **Par-<u>duhn</u>**

90. Please excuse me. (sorry)  *Excusez-moi.*
**Ecks-<u>kyoo-zay</u> mwah**

91. Excuse me! (to get someone's attention)  *Excusez-moi!*
**Ecks-<u>kyoo-zay</u> mwah**

92. Fantastic!  *Formidable!*  **Fore-mee-<u>dah</u>-bluh**

93. Unbelievable!  *Incroyable!*  **Ihn-kroy-<u>ah</u>-bluh**

94. Incredible! (to express disgust)  *Ça alors!*  **<u>Sah</u> ah-lore**

95. Marvelous!  *Magnifique!*  **<u>Mehn</u>-ee-<u>feek</u>**

96. Can I help you?  *Je peux vous aider?*
**Zhuh poo <u>vooz</u> ay-day**

97. Please come in.
*Entrez, s'il vous plaît. (formal)*
*Entre, s'il te plaît. (informal)*
**<u>Ehn</u>-tray see voo play**  **<u>Ehn</u>-tray seel tuh play**

98. Come here.
    *Venez, s'il vous plaît. (formal)    Viens, s'il te plaît. (informal)*
    **Vuh-nay see voo play    Vyihn seel tuh play**

99. I am in a hurry.    *Je suis pressé. (m.)    Je suis pressée. (f.)*
    **Zhuh swee press-say    Zhuh swee press-say**

100. I am late.    *Je suis en retard.*    **Zhuh swee ehn ruh-tar**

101. I am hungry.    *J'ai faim.*    **Zhay fihm**

102. I am thirsty.    *J'ai soif.*    **Zhay swahf**

103. I am tired.    *Je suis fatigué. (m.)    Je suis fatiguée. (f.)*
     **Zhuh swee fah-tee-gay    Zhuh swee fah-tee-gay**

104. I am sorry.    *Je suis désolé. (m.)    Je suis désolée. (f.)*
     **Zhuh swee day-zoh-lay    Zhuh swee day-zoh-lay**

105. What's wrong?    *Qu'est-qu'il y a?*    **Kess keel yah**

106. Is something the matter?    *Qu'est-ce qui ne va pas?*
     **Kess kee nuh vah pah**

107. It's ok.    *Ça va.*    **Sah vah**

108. I know.    *Je sais.*    **Zhuh say**

109. I don't know.    *Je ne sais pas.*    **Zhuh nuh say pah**

110. That's all.    *C'est tout.*    **Say too**

111. It doesn't matter.    *Ça ne fait rien.*    **Sah nuh fay ree-ehn**

112. It's not serious.    *C'est pas grave.*    **Say pah grahv**

113. Can you help me?    *Vous pouvez m'aider?*
     **Voo poo-vay may-day**

114. Can you tell me?    *Vous pouvez me le dire?*
     **Voo poo-vay muh luh deer**

115. Where is the restroom?    *Où sont les toilettes?*
     **Oo sone lay twah-let**

116. Leave me alone!    *Laissez-moi tranquille!*
     **Lay-say mwah tran-kee**

117.  I am looking for . . .    *Je cherche* . . .    Zhuh <u>share-sh</u>
 . . . my hotel.    . . . *mon hôtel.*    . . . mohn oh-<u>tell</u>
 . . . the train station.    . . . *la gare.*    . . . lah gahr
 . . . a restaurant.    . . . *un restaurant.*
 . . . uhn ress-toh-<u>rehn</u>
 . . . a bank    . . . *une banque.*    . . . oon <u>behn</u>-kuh

118.  Who?    *Qui?*    Kee

119.  What?    *Quoi?*    Kwah

120.  Why?    *Pourquoi?*    Por-<u>kwah</u>

121.  Where?    *Où?*    Oo

122.  When?    *Quand?*    Kehn

123.  How much?    *Combien?*    Kum-<u>byehn</u>

124.  How long/much time?    *Combien de temps?*
 Kum-<u>byehn</u> duh <u>tehn</u>

125.  To.    *À.*    Ah

126.  From.    *De.*    Duh

127.  With.    *Avec.*    Ah-<u>vek</u>

128.  Without.    *Sans.*    Sehn

129.  In.    *Dans.*    Dehn

130.  On.    *Sur.*    Soor

131.  Near.    *Près de.*    Pray duh

132.  Far.    *Loin de.*    Lwehn duh

133.  In front of.    *Devant.*    Duh-<u>vehn</u>

134.  Behind.    *Derrière.*    Dare-<u>ee-air</u>

135.  Next to.    *À côté de.*    Ah <u>koh-tay</u> duh

136.  Outside.    *À l'extérieur.*    Ah <u>lecks</u>-tare-ee-<u>er</u>

137. Inside.   *À l'intérieur.*   **Ah <u>lehn</u>-tare-ee-<u>er</u>**

138. Empty.   *Vide.*   **Veed**

139. Full.   *Plein. (m.)*   *Pleine. (f.)*   **Plihn   Plen**

140. Something.   *Quelque chose.*   **Kell-<u>kuh</u> shows**

141. Nothing.   *Rien.*   **Ree-ehn**

142. Several.   *Plusieurs.*   **Ploo-zyer**

143. (Much) more.   *(Beaucoup) plus.*   **(<u>Boh</u>-koo) <u>ploos</u>**

144. Less.   *Moins.*   **Mwehn**

145. (A little) more.   *(Un peu) plus.*   **(Uhn puh) <u>ploos</u>**

146. Enough.   *Assez.*   **ah-say**

147. Too much.   *Trop.*   **Troh**

148. Many.   *Beaucoup.*   **<u>Boh</u>-koo**

149. Very.   *Très.*   **Tray**

150. Good.   *Bon. (m.)*   *Bonne. (f.)*   **Bohn   Buhn**

151. Bad.   *Mauvais. (m.)*   *Mauvaise. (f.)*
     **<u>Moh</u>-vay   <u>Moh</u>-vehz**

152. Now.   *Maintenant.*   **Mihn-tuh-<u>nehn</u>**

153. Later.   *Plus tard.*   **<u>Ploo</u> tar**

154. Immediately.   *Tout de suite.*   **<u>Toot</u> sweet**

155. Soon.   *Bientôt.*   **<u>Byehn</u>-tow**

156. As soon as possible.   *Dès que possible.*
     **Day kuh poh-<u>seeb</u>-luh**

157. It is (too) late.   *Il est (trop) tard.*   **Eel ay (<u>troh</u>) tar**

158. It is (too) early.   *Il est (trop) tôt.*   **Eel ay (<u>troh</u>) tow**

159. Slowly. *Lentement.* <u>Lehn</u>-tuh-mehn

160. Slower. *Plus lentement.* <u>Ploo</u> lehn-tuh-mehn

161. Quickly. *Vite.* **Veet**

162. Quicker. *Plus vite.* **<u>Ploo</u> veet**

163. Look out! *Attention!* **Ah-<u>tehn</u>-syion**

164. Listen! *Écoutez!* **Ay-koo-<u>tay</u>**

165. Look! *Regardez!* **Ruh-gahr-<u>day</u>**

## DESCRIBING YOURSELF AND OTHERS

166. What does he look like? *Comment est-il?* **Kuh-muh et <u>eel</u>**

167. Can you describe him/her? *Pouvez-vous le / la décrire?*
**Poo-vay-voo luh / lah <u>day-kreer</u>**

168. He is young / old. *Il est jeune / vieux.*
**Eel ay zhuhn / vee-yuh**

169. She is (quite) young / old. *Elle est (très) jeune / vielle.*
**Ell ay (tray) <u>zhun</u> / <u>vee-yay</u>**

170. He has ... eyes. *Il a les yeux ...* **Eel ah lays yuh ...**

| | | |
|---|---|---|
| blue. | *bleus.* | **<u>bluh</u>** |
| green. | *verts.* | **<u>vair</u>** |
| brown. | *marron.* | **mah-<u>ruhn</u>** |
| hazel. | *noisette.* | **<u>nwah</u>-zet** |
| gray. | *gris.* | **<u>gree</u>** |

171. She has ... hair. *Elle a les cheveux ...*
**Ell ah lay shuh-vuh ...**

| | | |
|---|---|---|
| brown. | *bruns.* | **<u>bruhn</u>** |
| gray. | *gris.* | **<u>gree</u>** |
| blond. | *blonds.* | **<u>blohn</u>** |
| red. | *roux.* | **<u>roo</u>** |

172.   He has ... hair.    *Il a des cheveux ...*
       Eel ah day shuh-vuh

       short.          *courts.*        <u>koor</u>
       long.           *longs.*         <u>lohn</u>
       straight.       *raides.*        <u>red</u>
       curly.          *bouclés.*       boo-<u>klay</u>

173.   She's a ...      *Elle est ...*    Ell ay
       redhead.        *rousse.*        <u>roose</u>
       blonde.         *blonde.*        <u>blohn</u>-duh
       brunette.       *brune.*         <u>broo</u>-nuh

174.   He's bald.    *Il est chauve.*    Eel ay <u>shoh</u>-vuh

175.   She has ...    *Elle a ...*    Ell ah
       freckles.    *des tâches de rousseur.*    day <u>tahsh</u> duh roo-suhr
       dimples.    *des fossettes.*    day <u>fus</u>-set

176.   He has a beard and a mustache.
       *Il porte une barbe et une moustache.*
       Eel port oon <u>barb</u> ay oon moo-<u>stash</u>

177.   I have ...    *J'ai ...*    Zhay
       a tattoo.    *un tatouage.*    uhn tah-<u>too-ahzh</u>
       piercings.    *des piercings.*    day <u>peer-sing</u>

178.   He/she is very tan.    *Il / elle est (très) bronzé(e).*
       Eel / ell ay tray <u>brone-zay</u>

179.   He/she is so beautiful.    *Il / elle est si beau / belle.*
       Eel / ell ay see <u>boh</u> / <u>bell</u>

180.   He / she is ugly.    *Il / elle est laid / laide.*
       Eel / ell ay <u>lay</u> / <u>led</u>

181.   He/she is of medium build.    *Il / elle est de taille moyenne.*
       Eel / ell ay duh ty <u>moy-enn</u>

182.   I am ...    *Je suis ...*    Zhuh swee ...
       ... tall.        *... grand(e).*    <u>grehn</u> / <u>grehn-duh</u>
       ... short.       *... petit (e).*    <u>puh-tee</u> / <u>puh-teet</u>

... (very) thin.  ... *(très) mince.*  **(tray)** <u>mihnse</u>

... (not very) fat.  ... *(pas très) gros(se).*
**(pah tray)** <u>grow</u> / <u>gross</u>

183. I weigh 70 kilos.  *Je pèse 72 kilos.*
**Zhuh pez swah-sohn-dooz** <u>kee</u>**-loh**

184. I'm 1.75 meters tall.  *Je mesure 1 mètre 75.*
**Zhuh muh-zoor uhn** <u>meh-truh</u> **swah-sohn-kihnz**

185. What a(n) ... child!  *Quel enfant ...!*  **Kell** <u>ehn-fehn</u>
adorable  *adorable*  **ah-dore-**<u>ah</u>**-bluh**
cute  *mignon*  <u>mee</u>**-nyion**

186. He / she is quite ...  *Il / elle est très ...*
**Eel / ell ay tray ...**
... serious.  ... *sérieux / sérieuse.*
<u>say</u>**-ree-uh** / <u>say</u>**-ree-uhz**
... funny.  ... *drôle.*  **drole**
... intelligent.  ... *intelligent (e)*
<u>ihn</u>**-tell-ee-**<u>zhehn</u> / <u>ihn</u>**-tell-ee-**<u>zhehn</u>**-tuh**

187. He / she isn't ...  *Il / elle n'est pas ...*  **Eel / ell nay pah**
mean.  *méchant(e).*  <u>may</u>**-shehn** / <u>may</u>**-shehn-tuh**
rude.  *impoli(e).*  <u>ihm</u>**-poh-lee**

188. He / she seems ...  *Il / elle a l'air ...*  **Eel / ell ah lair**
... calm.  ... *calme.*  <u>kahl</u>**-muh**
... happy.  ... *heureux.*  **er-**<u>ruh</u>
... depressed.  ... *déprimé.*  <u>day</u>**-pree-**<u>may</u>

# DIFFICULTIES

189. I cannot find my hotel address.
*Je ne peux pas trouver l'adresse de mon hôtel.*
**Zhuh nuh puh pah troo-vay lah-**<u>dress</u> **duh mohn oh-**<u>tell</u>

190. Can you help me?  *Vous pouvez m'aider?*
**Voo poo-vay** <u>may-day</u>

191. Help! (in case of an emergency)    *Au secours!*
     Oh <u>suh-koor</u>

192. I have lost . . .    *J'ai perdu . . .*    Zhay pair-<u>doo</u>
     . . . my keys.          . . . *mes clés.*        may klay
     . . . my passport.    . . . *mon passeport.*    mohn <u>pass</u>-pore

193. Right now I'm looking for . . .
     *Je suis en train de chercher . . .*
     Zhuh swee zehn trehn duh <u>share</u>-shay
     . . . my wallet.      . . . *mon portefeuille.*    mohn <u>por</u>-tuh-foy
     . . . my purse.      . . . *mon sac à main.*      mohn <u>sak</u>-ah-man
     . . . my ticket.     . . . *mon billet.*          mohn <u>bee</u>-yay

194. Have you seen . . . ?    *Avez-vous vu . . . ?*    Ah-vay voo <u>vooh</u>
     . . . my husband    . . . *mon mari*    mohn mah-<u>ree</u>
     . . . my wife        . . . *ma femme*    mah <u>fahm</u>

195. I forgot my money.    *J'ai oublié mon argent.*
     Zhay oo-blee-yay mohn <u>ar</u>-zhehn

196. I have missed my train.    *J'ai manqué mon train.*
     Zhay mehn-kay mohn <u>trehn</u>

197. What should I do?    *Que dois-je faire?*
     Kuh dwah-zhuh <u>fair</u>

198. Can you help me contact . . . ?
     *Pouvez-vous m'aider à contacter . . . ?*
     Poo-vay voo may-day ah <u>kone</u>-tahk-tay
     . . . my famille    . . . *ma famille*    mah fah-<u>mee</u>
     . . . my colleague    . . . *mon (m.) / ma (f.) collègue*
     mohn <u>koll</u>-eg    mah <u>koll</u>-eg

199. My glasses are broken.    *Mes lunettes sont cassées.*
     May loo-net sohn <u>ka</u>-say

200. Where can I get them repaired?
     *Où peut-on les faire réparer?*
     Oo puh-tuhn lay fair <u>ray</u>-pah-<u>ray</u>

201.   I need a new hearing aid.
       *J'ai besoin d'un nouvel appareil acoustique.*
       **Zhay buh-zwehn duhn noo-vell <u>ah</u>-pah-ray <u>ah-koo</u>-steek**

202.   This is my medication.     *Voici mes médicaments.*
       **Vwa-see may <u>may-dee</u>-kah-<u>mehn</u>**

203.   Where is the lost-and-found desk?
       *Où se trouve le bureau des objets trouvés?*
       **Oo suh troov luh <u>boo</u>-roh daze <u>ub-zhay</u> troo-<u>vay</u>**

204.   Is the American consulate nearby?
       *Est-ce que le consulat des États-Unis est près d'ici?*
       **Ess kuh luh kone-suh-<u>lah</u> daze ay-tahz ay oo-<u>nee</u> pray dee-<u>see</u>**

205.   I'm looking for the police station.
       *Je cherche la station de police.*
       **Zhuh <u>share-sh</u> lah stah-<u>see-yion</u> duh <u>poh</u>-lees**

206.   I am going to call a policeman.
       *Je vais appeler un agent de police.*
       **Zhuh vaze <u>ah-pull-ay</u> uhn azh-ehn duh <u>poh</u>-lees**

## NUMBERS AND TELLING TIME

In France and most other French-speaking countries, the 24-hour clock, or *l'heure officielle*, is used for transportation schedules as well as other official situations. Seven o'clock in the morning would be written in *l'heure conventionnelle* as 7h00, whereas seven o'clock at night would be 19h00. An easy way to convert from the 24-hour clock to the American convention of telling time is to subtract 12.

207.   One.      *Un.*       Uhn

208.   Two.      *Deux.*     Duh

209.   Three.    *Trois.*    Twah

210.   Four.     *Quatre.*   Kaht

211.   Five.     *Cinq.*     Sank

| | | |
|---|---|---|
| 212. | Six. | *Six.* | **Sees** |
| 213. | Seven. | *Sept.* | **Set** |
| 214. | Eight. | *Huit.* | **Weet** |
| 215. | Nine. | *Neuf.* | **Nuff** |
| 216. | Ten. | *Dix.* | **Dees** |
| 217. | Eleven. | *Onze.* | **Ownz** |
| 218. | Twelve. | *Douze.* | **Dooz** |
| 219. | Thirteen. | *Treize.* | **Trayze** |
| 220. | Fourteen. | *Quatorze.* | **Kah-torze** |
| 221. | Fifteen. | *Quinze.* | **Kehnze** |
| 222. | Sixteen. | *Seize.* | **Sez** |
| 223. | Seventeen. | *Dix-sept.* | **Dee-set** |
| 224. | Eighteen. | *Dix-huit.* | **Dee-zweet** |
| 225. | Nineteen. | *Dix-neuf.* | **Dee-znuff** |
| 226. | Twenty. | *Vingt.* | **Vihn** |
| 227. | Twenty-one. | *Vingt-et-un.* | **Vihn-tay-uhn** |
| 228. | Twenty-two. | *Vingt-deux.* | **Vihn-duh** |
| 229. | Twenty-three. | *Vingt-trois.* | **Vihn-twah** |
| 230. | Twenty-four. | *Vingt-quatre.* | **Vihn-kaht** |

231. What time is it?    *Quelle heure est-il?*    **Kell er et eel**

232. It is seven o'clock.    *Il est sept heures.*    **Eel ay set er**

233. It is nine o'clock in the morning.
*Il est neuf heures du matin.*    **Eel ay nuff er doo ma-tan**

234. Is it three-thirty?    *Il est trois heures et demie?*
**Eel ay twa zer ay duh-mee**

235. No, it's three forty-five.
*Non, il est quatre heures moins le quart.*
Noh eel ay <u>kaht</u> rer mwehn luh kar

236. It's noon.   *Il est midi.*   Eel ay <u>mee</u>-dee

237. It's midnight.   *Il est minuit.*   Eel ay <u>mee</u>-nwee

238. My train is at quarter to ten.
*Mon train part à dix heures moins dix.*
Mohn trehn par ah <u>dee</u> <u>zer</u> mwehn dees

239. At ten minutes past seven.   *À sept heures dix.*
Ah <u>set</u> er dees

# TALKING ABOUT DAYS OF THE WEEK AND MONTHS

240. Today.   *Aujourd'hui.*   Oh-zhoor-<u>dwee</u>

241. Tomorrow.   *Demain.*   Duh-<u>mihn</u>

242. Yesterday.   *Hier.*   Ee-<u>yair</u>

243. Week.   *Semaine.*   Suh-<u>men</u>

244. See you tomorrow!   *À demain!*   Ah <u>duh</u>-mihn

245. Next week.   *La semaine prochaine.*
Lah suh-<u>men</u> pro-<u>shen</u>

246. See you next week!   *À la semaine prochaine!*
Ah lah suh-<u>men</u> pro-<u>shen</u>

247. Last week.   *La semaine dernière.*   Lah <u>suh-men</u> dare-nyair

248. Day.   *Le jour.*   Luh zhoor

249. Month.   *Le mois.*   Luh mwah

250. Year.   *L'année.*   Lah-<u>nay</u>

251. Next year.   *L'année prochaine.*   Lah-<u>nay</u> pro-<u>shen</u>

252. See you next year!   *À l'année prochaine!*
Ah lah-<u>nay</u> pro-<u>shen</u>

253. Last year.    *L'année dernière.*    **Lah-nay dare-nyair**

254. We met each other last year.
*On s'est rencontrés l'année dernière.*
**Ohn say rehn-kehn-tray lah-nay dare-nyair**

255. I work on . . .    *Je travaille . . .*    **Zhuh trah-vy**

| | | |
|---|---|---|
| Mondays. | *le lundi.* | luh **luhn**-dee |
| Tuesdays. | *le mardi.* | luh **mar**-dee |
| Wednesdays. | *le mercredi.* | luh **mare**-cruh-dee |
| Thursdays. | *le jeudi.* | luh **zhuh**-dee |
| Fridays. | *le vendredi.* | luh **vehn**-druh-dee |
| Saturdays. | *le samedi.* | luh **sahm**-dee |
| Sundays. | *le dimanche.* | luh dee-**mehn-sh** |

256. I have a meeting this Saturday.    *J'ai une réunion samedi.*
**Zhay oon ray-yoon-yuhn sahm-dee**

257. What day is it today?    *Quel jour sommes-nous?*
**Kell zhoor summ noo**

258. Today is Friday.    *Aujourd'hui on est vendredi.*
**Oh-zhoor-dwee ohn ay vehn-druh-dee**

259. I'll be in Paris next . . .    *Je serai à Paris . . . prochain.*
**Zuh suh-ray ah pah-ree . . . pro-shihn**

| | | |
|---|---|---|
| January. | *le janvier.* | luh **zhehn**-vee-yay |
| February. | *le février.* | luh **fay**-vree-yay |
| March. | *le mars.* | luh marse |
| April. | *l'avril.* | lahv-**reel** |
| May. | *le mai.* | luh may |
| June. | *le juin.* | luh zhwehn |
| July. | *le juillet.* | luh **zhwee**-yay |
| August. | *l'août.* | **loot** |
| September. | *le septembre.* | luh say-**tahm**-bruh |
| October. | *l'octobre.* | lok-**toh**-bruh |

November.       *le novembre.*      luh no-<u>vahm</u>-bruh
December.       *le décembre.*      luh day-<u>sem</u>-bruh

260.  Our appointment is for March 4th.
      *Notre rendez-vous est pour le quatre mars.*
      Note <u>rehn</u>-day-voo ay poor luh <u>kaht</u> marse

261.  Next month.    *Le mois prochain.*    Luh <u>mwah</u> pro-<u>shihn</u>

262.  Last month.    *Le mois dernier.*    Luh mwah dare-<u>nyay</u>

263.  When is your birthday? (formal)
      *Quelle est la date de votre anniversaire?*
      Kell ay lah daht duh <u>vote</u> ehn-ee-vair-<u>sair</u>

264.  When is your birthday? (informal)
      *C'est quand ton anniversaire?*
      Say <u>kehn</u> tone ehn-ee-vair-<u>sair</u>

265.  My birthday is April 16th.
      *Mon anniversaire, c'est le seize avril.*
      <u>Mohn</u> ehn-ee-vair-<u>sair</u> say luh <u>sez</u> ahv-<u>reel</u>

# TALKING ABOUT THE WEATHER AND SEASONS

266.  What's the weather like today?
      *Quel temps fait-il aujourd'hui?*
      Kell <u>tehn</u> fate eel oh-<u>zhoor</u>-dwee

267.  What's the forecast for tomorrow?
      *Quelle est la météo pour demain?*
      Kell ay lah <u>may-tay</u>-oh poor duh-<u>mihn</u>

268.  I love the climate here.    *J'aime bien le climat ici.*
      Zhem <u>byehn</u> luh klee-<u>mah</u> ee-see

269.  Back home it's . . .    *Chez moi . . .*    Shay mwah

      . . . sunnier.    . . . *c'est plus ensoleillé.*
      say plooz <u>ehn</u>-soh-lay-<u>yay</u>
      . . . more humid.    . . . *il fait plus humide.*
      eel fay <u>plooz</u> oo-<u>meed</u>
      . . . hotter.    . . . *il fait plus chaud.*    eel fay ploo <u>shoh</u>

270. It's sunny.    *Il fait du soleil.*    Eel fay doo <u>soh</u>-<u>lay</u>

271. It's cloudy.    *Le ciel est couvert.*    Luh see-yell ay <u>koo</u>-vair

272. It's windy.    *Il y a du vent.*    Eel ya doo <u>vehn</u>

273. It's cold.    *Il fait froid.*    Eel fay <u>fwah</u>

274. It's hot.    *Il fait chaud.*    Eel fay <u>shoh</u>

275. What a heatwave!    *Quelle canicule!*    Kell kehn-ee-<u>kool</u>

276. It's (very) chilly.    *Il fait (très) frais.*    Eel fay (tray) <u>fray</u>

277. It's snowing.    *Il neige.*    Eel <u>nehzh</u>

278. It's raining.    *Il pleut.*    Eel <u>pluh</u>

279. The weather is dreadful!    *Il fait un temps épouvantable!*
Eel fay uhn tehn <u>ay</u>-poo-vehnt-<u>ab-luh</u>

280. What's your favorite season?
*Quelle est votre saison préférée?*
Kell ay <u>vote</u> say-zon pray-fay-<u>ray</u>

281. I prefer . . .    *Moi je préfère . . .*    Mwah zhuh pray-<u>fair</u>
     Winter.          *L'hiver.*          <u>lee</u>-vair
     Spring.          *Le printemps.*     luh <u>prihn</u>-tehn
     Summer.          *L'été.*            <u>lay</u>-tay
     Fall.            *L'automne.*        <u>loh</u>-tuhn

282. I really dislike . . .    *Personnellement je déteste . . .*
Pair-sun-ell-<u>mehn</u> zhuh <u>day</u>-test
     . . . the heat.    . . . *la chaleur.*    lah <u>shah</u>-ler
     . . . the cold.    . . . *le froid.*     luh <u>fwah</u>

283. Next summer.    *L'été prochain.*    Lay-<u>tay</u> pro-<u>shihn</u>

284. Last fall.    *L'automne dernier.*    Loh-<u>tuhn</u> dare-<u>nyay</u>

# Chapter 2
## Travel

## TRAVEL: GENERAL VOCABULARY AND EXPRESSIONS

285. Excuse me, where is . . . ?  *Excusez-moi, où se trouve . . . ?*
**Ecks-kyoo-zay mwah oo suh troov**

. . . downtown.  *. . . le centre-ville.*  **luh <u>sehn</u>-truh <u>veel</u>**

. . . the shopping district.
*. . . le quartier / le centre commercial.*
**luh <u>kar</u>-tee-yay / luh <u>sehn</u>-truh ko-mer-see-<u>ahl</u>**

. . . the residential neighborhood.  *. . . le quartier résidentiel.*
**luh <u>kar</u>-tee-yay rez-ee-dehn-see-<u>yell</u>**

286. Is this the right direction?  *Est-ce la bonne direction?*
**Ess lah <u>buhn</u> dee-rek-<u>syuhn</u>**

287. Where is it?  *Où est-ce?*  **Oo ess**

288. To the right?  *À gauche?*  **Ah <u>goh</u>-sh**

289. To the left?  *À droite?*  **Ah <u>dwaht</u>**

290. Is it on this side of the street?  *Est-ce de ce côté de la rue?*
**Ess duh <u>suh</u> koh-tay duh lah <u>roo</u>**

291. Is it on the other side of the street?
*Est-ce de l'autre côté de la rue?*
**Ess duh <u>lohte</u> koh-tay duh lah <u>roo</u>**

292. At the corner?  *Au coin de la rue? Au coin des rues + . . . ?*
**Oh <u>kwehn</u> duh lah <u>roo</u> / oh <u>kwehn</u> day <u>roo</u> (+ names)**

293. Across the street?    *En face?*    **Ehn <u>fahs</u>**

294. In the middle?    *Au milieu?*    **Oh meel-<u>ew</u>**

295. Straight ahead?    *Tout droit?*    **Too <u>dwah</u>**

296. Forward.    *Avant / En avant.*    **Ah-<u>vehn</u> / Ehn ah-<u>vehn</u>**

297. Back.    *Arrière / En arrière.*    **Ah-ree-<u>yair</u> / Ehn <u>ah</u>-ree-<u>yair</u>**

298. In front of.    *En face de.*    **Ehn fahs <u>duh</u>**

299. Behind.    *Derrière.*    **Dare-ee-<u>yair</u>**

300. Next to.    *À côté de.*    **Ah koh-tay <u>duh</u>**

301. To the right of.    *À la droite de.*    **Ah lah <u>dwaht</u> <u>duh</u>**

302. To the left of.    *À la gauche de.*    **Ah lah <u>goh-sh</u> <u>duh</u>**

303. To the north.    *Au nord.*    **Oh <u>nor</u>**

304. To the south.    *Au sud.*    **Oh s<u>ood</u>**

305. To the east.    *À l'est.*    **Ah <u>lest</u>**

306. To the west.    *À l'ouest.*    **Ah luh-<u>west</u>**

307. What is the address?    *Quelle est l'adresse?*
     **Kell ay lah-<u>dress</u>**

308. What street is this?    *On est dans quelle rue?*
     **Ohn ay dehn kell <u>roo</u>**

309. Where is the nearest travel agency?
     *Où est l'agence de voyage la plus proche?*
     **Oo ay lah-<u>zhens</u> duh voy-<u>ahzh</u> lah ploo <u>proh-sh</u>**

310. Can you help me make a reservation?
     *Pourriez-vous m'aider à faire une réservation?*
     **Poo-ree-yay voo <u>may</u>-day ah fair oon <u>ray</u>-zair-vah-<u>syion</u>**

311. How long is the trip between . . . and . . . ?
     *Cela prend combien de temps pour aller de . . . à . . . ?*
     **Suh-lah <u>prehn</u> kum-<u>byehn</u> duh <u>tehn</u> poor ah-lay duh . . . ah . . .**

312. Where can I get a (train) schedule?
*Où puis-je trouver les horaires (de train)?*
**Oo pwee zhuh troo-vay laze <u>or-air</u> (duh trehn)**

313. Will I need my passport?
*Est-ce que j'aurai besoin de mon passeport?*
**Ess kuh zhohr-ay <u>buh</u>-zwehn duh mohn pass-<u>por</u>**

314. Do I need a visa to visit this country?
*Est-ce que je dois avoir un visa pour visiter ce pays?*
**Ess kuh zhuh dwah <u>zahv-wahr</u> uhn vee-<u>za</u> pohr vee-zee-tay
suh <u>payee</u>**

315. I missed . . .    *J'ai manqué* . . .    zhay <u>mehn</u>-kay

. . . my flight.    . . . *mon vol.*    mohn <u>vuhl</u>

. . . my train.    . . . *mon train.*    mohn <u>trehn</u>

. . . my local bus.    . . . *mon bus.*    mohn <u>boos</u>

. . . my intercity bus.    . . . *mon car.*    mohn <u>kar</u>

. . . my shuttle.    . . . *ma navette.*    mah nah-<u>vet</u>

. . . my ride.    . . . *mon moyen de transport.*
mon mwa-<u>yen</u> duh trehn-<u>spore</u>

# TICKETS

316. Ticket.    *Le billet.*    Luh bee-<u>yay</u>

317. First class.    *Première classe.*    <u>Pruh</u>-me-yair <u>klahss</u>

318. Second class.    *Deuxième classe.*    <u>Duh</u>-zee-yem <u>klahss</u>

319. A reserved seat.    *Une place réservée.*
Oon <u>plahs</u> <u>ray</u>-zair-<u>vay</u>

320. Discounted rate ticket.    *Un billet à tarif réduit.*
Uhn bee-<u>yay</u> ah tah-<u>reef</u> ray-<u>dwee</u>

321. Group rate.    *Un tarif de groupe.*    Uhn tah-<u>reef</u> duh <u>groop</u>

322. Student discount.    *Un tarif étudiant.*
Uhn tah-<u>reef</u> ay-too-<u>dyehn</u>

323. Senior discount.     *Un tarif troisième âge.*
Uhn tah-<u>reef</u> twa-zyem <u>ahzh</u>

324. I need to go to the Air France ticket counter.
*J'ai besoin d'aller au comptoir Air France.*
Zhay <u>buh</u>-zwehn <u>dah</u>-lay oh con-<u>twahr</u> air <u>frehns</u>

325. How much does this ticket cost?     *Combien coûte ce billet?*
Kum-<u>byehn</u> koot suh <u>bee</u>-yay

326. Where is the ticket window?     *Où est le guichet?*
Oo <u>ay</u> luh <u>gee</u>-shay

327. I'd like to buy a one-way ticket.
*Je voudrais acheter un billet simple.*
Zhuh voo-dray <u>ahsh</u>-tay uhn <u>bee</u>-yay <u>sihm</u>-pluh

328. I'd like to buy a round-trip ticket.
*Je voudrais acheter un billet aller-retour.*
Zhuh voo-dray <u>ahsh</u>-tay uhn <u>bee</u>-yay  ah-lay-<u>ruh</u>-toor

329. I'd like a first-class ticket.
*Je voudrais un billet première classe.*
Zhuh voo-dray uhn <u>bee</u>-yay <u>pruh</u>-myair <u>klahss</u>

330. Is this ticket refundable?     *Est-ce un billet remboursable?*
Ess uhn <u>bee</u>-yay rahm-boor-<u>sahm</u>-bluh

331. Is it possible to change dates?
*Est-il possible de changer de dates?*
Et-eel puhs-<u>see</u>-bluh duh <u>shehn</u>-zhay duh <u>daht</u>

332. Is it possible to have another seat?
*Est-ce que c'est possible d'avoir un siège différent?*
Ess-kuh say puhs-<u>see</u>-bluh <u>dahv</u>-wahr uhn see-<u>yezh</u>
deef-fay-<u>rehn</u>

333. I would like a seat . . .     *Je voudrais un siège . . .*
Zhuh voo-<u>dray</u> uhn see-<u>yezh</u>

. . . next to my husband.     . . . *à côté de mon mari.*
ah <u>koh</u>-tay duh <u>mohn</u> mah-<u>ree</u>

. . . next to my wife.     . . . *à côté de ma femme.*
ah <u>koh</u>-tay duh <u>mah</u> <u>fahm</u>

. . . next to the window.     . . . *côté fenêtre.*
<u>koh</u>-tay fuh-<u>net</u>-ruh

. . . next to the aisle.     . . . *côté couloir.*
<u>koh</u>-tay <u>koo</u>-lwahr

334. Can I book a reservation on line?
*Est-ce que je peux réserver en ligne?*
Ess-<u>kuh</u> zhuh puh <u>ray</u>-zair-<u>vay</u> ehn lee-<u>nyuh</u>

335. Is this an e-ticket?     *Est-ce un billet électronique?*
Ess uhn <u>bee</u>-yay ay-lek-troh-<u>neek</u>

336. May I have a copy of my itinerary?
*Puis-je avoir une copie de mon itinéraire?*
Pwee-zhahv-<u>wahr</u> oon koh-<u>pee</u> duh mone ee-tin-ay-<u>rair</u>

# TRAVELING BY CAR

337. A car.     *Une voiture.*     Oon <u>vwah</u>-toor

338. A car rental agency.     *Une agence de location de voitures.*
Oon ah-<u>zhance</u> duh low-kah-see-<u>yon</u> duh <u>vwah</u>-toor

339. I'd like to rent a car.     *J'aimerais louer une voiture.*
Zhem-<u>ray</u> loo-ay oon <u>vwah</u>-toor

340. What are your rates?     *Quels sont vos tarifs?*
Kell <u>sohn</u> voh tah-<u>reef</u>

341. Do I need to pay a deposit?     *Faut-il verser un acompte?*
Foh-<u>teel</u> vair-<u>say</u> uhn ah-<u>conte</u>

342. A driver's license.     *Un permis de conduire.*
Uhn pair-<u>mee</u> duh kuhn-<u>dweer</u>

343. Do I need an international driver's license?
*Est-ce que j'ai besoin d'un permis de conduire international?*
Ess-kuh zhay <u>buh</u>-zwehn <u>duhn</u> pair-<u>mee</u> duh kuhn-<u>dweer</u>
ihn-tern-ah-syion-<u>al</u>

344. Comprehensive insurance.     *L'assurance tous-risques.*
Lah-soo-<u>rehnce</u> too-<u>rees</u>-kuh

345. Does this price include comprehensive insurance?
*Est-ce que ce prix comprend l'assurance tous-risques?*
**Ess-kuh <u>suh</u> pree kom-<u>prehn</u> lah-soo-<u>rehnce</u> too-<u>rees</u>-kuh**

346. To drive.   *Conduire.*   **Kuhn-<u>dweer</u>**

347. I am driving from Sète to Pau.
*Je conduis de Sète à Pau.*   **Zhuh kuhn-<u>dwee</u> duh <u>set</u> ah <u>poh</u>**

348. Do you have a map of the area?
*Avez-vous un plan de la région?*
**Ah-vay-<u>voo</u> uhn <u>plehn</u> duh lah <u>ray</u>-zhee-on**

349. Where is the nearest gas station?
*Où est la station-service la plus proche?*
**Oo ay lah stah-<u>see-yion</u> sehr-<u>vees</u> lah ploo <u>proh-sh</u>**

350. Fill it up, please.   *Le plein, s'il vous plaît.*
**Luh <u>plihn</u> see voo <u>play</u>**

351. Can you check the air in the tires?
*Pouvez-vous vérifier la pression des pneus?*
**Poo-vay voo <u>vay</u>-ree-<u>fyay</u> lah <u>press</u>-syion day <u>puh-nuh</u>**

352. I need to have my car fixed.
*J'ai besoin de faire réparer ma voiture.*
**Zhay <u>buh</u>-zwehn <u>duh</u> fare ray-pah-<u>ray</u> mah <u>vwah</u>-toor**

353. My car is broken down.   *Ma voiture est en panne.*
**Mah <u>vwah</u>-toor ay tuhn <u>pehn</u>**

354. I can't start the car.   *Je ne peux pas démarrer la voiture.*
**Zhuh nuh <u>puh</u> pah <u>day</u>-mah-ray lah <u>vwah</u>-toor**

355. The battery is dead.   *La batterie est à plat.*
**Lah <u>bah</u>-tree et ah <u>plah</u>**

356. I am out of gas.   *Je suis en panne d'essence.*
**<u>Zhuh</u> swee zehn pehn dess-<u>ehnce</u>**

357. I have a flat tire.   *J'ai un pneu crevé.*
**Zhay uhn <u>puh-nuh</u> kruh-<u>vay</u>**

358. The engine is overheating.   *Le moteur chauffe.*
**Luh moh-<u>tuhr</u> shoh-ff**

359. I think it needs water.    *Je crois qu'il lui faut de l'eau.*
Zhuh <u>kwah</u> keel lwee <u>foh</u> duh <u>loh</u>

360. There is a leak.    *Il y a une fuite.*    Eel <u>ya</u> oon <u>fweet</u>

361. Is there a garage nearby?
*Est-ce qu'il y a un garage près d'ici?*
Ess keel <u>ya</u> uhn gah-<u>razh</u> preh dee-<u>see</u>

362. Can you tow me to the nearest garage?
*Pouvez-vous me remorquer jusqu'au garage le plus proche?*
Poo-vay voo <u>muh</u> ruh-more-<u>kay</u> zhoo-sk <u>oh</u> gah-<u>razh</u> luh
ploo <u>proh-sh</u>

# AIR TRAVEL

363. Airport.    *L'aéroport.*    **Lair-oh-<u>pore</u>**

364. How can I get to the airport?
*Comment je fais pour aller à l'aéroport?*
Kuh-<u>muh</u> zhuh <u>fay</u> poor ah-<u>lay</u> ah lair-oh-<u>pore</u>

365. Is this there a shuttle for the airport?
*Il y a une navette pour l'aéroport?*
Eel <u>ya</u> oon nah-<u>vet</u> poor lair-oh-<u>pore</u>

366. Airline.    *La compagnie de vol.*
Lah <u>comb</u>-pah-<u>nee</u> duh <u>vuhl</u>

367. I am flying on Air France.    *Je prends un vol Air France.*
Zhuh <u>prehn</u> uhn <u>vuhl</u> air-<u>frehnse</u>

368. Where do I check my bags?
*Où est-ce que je peux enregistrer mes bagages?*
<u>Oo</u> ess kuh zhuh puh <u>ehn</u>-ruh-zhees-<u>tray</u> may bah-<u>gahzh</u>

369. I'd like to confirm my reservation on . . .
*J'aimerais confirmer ma réservation sur le vol . . .*
Zhem-<u>ray</u> cone-feer-<u>may</u> mah <u>ray</u>-zair-vah-<u>syion</u> soor luh <u>vuhl</u>

370. Do I need a boarding pass?
*Est-ce qu'il me faut une carte d'embarquement?*
Ess <u>keel</u> muh <u>foh</u> oon <u>kart</u> duhm-bark-<u>mehn</u>

371.   My flight is leaving at 7:45 in the morning.
       *Mon vol part à 7h45. (sept heures quarante-cinq)*
       Mohn <u>vuhl</u> pahr ah <u>set</u>-er-kah-rehn-<u>sank</u>

372.   Is the flight late?     *Est-ce que le vol a du retard?*
       Ess kuh luh <u>vuhl</u> ah doo ruh-<u>tar</u>

373.   When is the next flight to Marrakech?
       *Le prochain vol pour Marrakech, c'est quand?*
       Luh proh-<u>shihn</u> vuhl poor <u>mah</u>-rah-kesh say <u>kehn</u>

374.   Is this a direct flight?     *Est-ce un vol direct?*
       Ess uhn <u>vuhl</u> dee-<u>rekt</u>

375.   How many bags may I check?
       *Je peux enregistrer combien de bagages?*
       Zhuh <u>puh</u> ehn-ruh-zhees-<u>tray</u> kum-<u>byehn</u> duh bah-<u>gahzh</u>

376.   Where is the check-in for my flight?
       *Où est l'enregistrement pour mon vol?*
       Oo ay <u>luhn</u>-ruh-zhee-struh-<u>mehn</u> poor mohn <u>vuhl</u>

377.   Where is the departure gate?
       *Où est la porte d'embarquement?*
       Oo ay lah <u>port</u> duhm-bark-<u>mehn</u>

378.   Can I bring this on board?     *Je peux apporter cela à bord?*
       Zhuh puh <u>ah</u>-pore-tay suh-lah ah <u>bore</u>

379.   Where is the baggage claim?     *Où est le retrait des bagages?*
       Oo ay luh ruh-<u>tray</u> day bah-<u>gahzh</u>

380.   Where is the luggage from the flight from . . . ?
       *Où sont les bagages du vol en provenance de . . . ?*
       Oo <u>sohn</u> lay bah-<u>gahzh</u> doo vuhl ehn pruhv-<u>nehnce</u> duh

381.   We have jet lag.     *Nous souffrons du décalage horaire.*
       Noo soo-<u>frehn</u> doo day-cah-<u>lahzh</u> ore-<u>rair</u>

## CUSTOMS AND BAGGAGE

382.   Where is the customs?     *Où est la douane?*
       Oo ay lah <u>dwahn</u>

383. Where is the passport check?
*Où est le contrôle des passeports?*
**Oo ay luh cone-<u>troll</u> day pass-<u>pore</u>**

384. I'm here on a stopover on my way to . . .
*Je fais escale en route pour . . .*
**Zhuh fay ess-<u>kahl</u> ehn root <u>poor</u>**

385. My passport.    *Mon passeport.*    **Mohn pass-<u>pore</u>**

386. Here are my bags.    *Voici mes bagages.*
**Vwa-see may bah-<u>gahzh</u>**

387. I have nothing to declare.    *Je n'ai rien à déclarer.*
**Zhuh nay ree-<u>ehn</u> ah <u>day</u>-klah-<u>ray</u>**

388. This is for my personal use.
*Ceci est pour mon usage personnel.*
**Suh-<u>see</u> ay poor mohn noo-<u>zahzh</u> pair-soh-<u>nell</u>**

389. How much do I pay?    *Je dois payer combien?*
**Zhuh dwah pay-<u>yay</u> kum-<u>byehn</u>**

390. I'd like to leave these bags at the baggage office.
*Je voudrais laisser ces bagages en consigne.*
**Zhuh voo-<u>dray</u> less-say say bah-<u>gahzh</u> ehn kuhn-<u>see-nyuh</u>**

# TRAVELING BY TRAIN

391. Train station.    *La gare.*    **Lah <u>gahr</u>**

392. Where is the train station?    *Où se trouve la gare?*
**Oo suh <u>troov</u> lah <u>gahr</u>**

393. When does the train for Calais leave?
*À quelle heure part le train pour Calais?*
**Ah kell <u>er</u> par luh <u>trehn</u> poor <u>kah</u>-leh**

394. The platforms are over there.    *L'accès aux quais est là-bas.*
**Lahk-<u>say</u> oh <u>kay</u> ay <u>lah</u>-bah**

395. Is this the right platform for the train to Brussels?
*Est-ce le bon quai pour le train pour Bruxelles?*
**Ess luh bohn <u>kay</u> poor luh <u>trehn</u> poor broo-<u>sell</u>**

396. Is this the train for Paris?    *Est-ce le train pour Paris?*
**Ess luh <u>trehn</u> poor pah-<u>ree</u>**

397. Is this the train from Paris?
*Est-ce le train en provenance de Paris?*
**Ess luh <u>trehn</u> ehn pruhv-<u>nehnce</u> duh pah-<u>ree</u>**

398. Does this train stop at Dijon?
*Est-ce que ce train s'arrête à Dijon?*
**Ess kuh suh <u>trehn</u> sah-<u>rett</u> ah dee-<u>zhon</u>**

399. Stamp your ticket.    *Composter votre billet.*
**Kuhm-poh-<u>stay</u> vote bee-<u>yay</u>**

400. What time does the train from Angers arrive?
*Le train en provenance d'Angers arrive à quelle heure?*
**Luh <u>trehn</u> ehn pruhv-<u>nehnce</u> <u>dehn</u>-zhay ah-<u>reev</u> ah kell <u>er</u>**

401. I'd like to buy a ticket on the TGV to Dijon.
*Je voudrais réserver une place dans le TGV pour Dijon.*
**Zhuh voo-<u>dray</u> ray-zair-<u>vay</u> oon <u>plahs</u> poor <u>luh</u>
tay-zhay-<u>vay</u> poor dee-<u>zhon</u>**

402. Is there a connection?    *Est-ce qu'il y a une correspondance?*
**Ess keel <u>ya</u> oon <u>core</u>-ess-pehn-<u>dehnce</u>**

403. How much time do I have to make the connection?
*Combien de temps est-ce que j'ai pour prendre la correspondance?*
**Kum-<u>byehn</u> duh <u>tehn</u> es kuh <u>zhay</u> poor <u>prehn</u>-druh lah
<u>core</u>-ess-pehn-<u>dehnce</u>**

404. We have to run to make our connection.
*On doit courir pour prendre notre correspondance.*
**Ohn dwah koo-<u>reer</u> poor note <u>core</u>-ess-pehn-<u>dehnce</u>**

405. We have two reserved seats.    *On a deux places réservées.*
**Oh nah <u>duh</u> plahs <u>ray</u>-zair-<u>vay</u>**

406. Tickets, please.    *Présentez vos billets, s'il vous plaît.*
**<u>Pray</u>-zehn-tay voh bee-<u>yay</u> see voo <u>play</u>**

407. This seat is taken.    *Cette place est prise.*
**Sett <u>plahs</u> ay <u>preez</u>**

408. Where is the dining car?    *Où est le wagon-restaurant?*
     Oo ay luh <u>vah</u>-guhn ress-toh-<u>rehn</u>

409. I almost missed my train.    *J'ai failli manqué mon train.*
     Zhay fie-<u>yee</u> mehn-<u>kay</u> mohn <u>trehn</u>

410. Does this train have Wi-Fi?
     *Est-ce que ce train a une borne Wi-Fi?*
     Ess kuh suh <u>trehn</u> ah oon <u>born</u> wee-<u>fee</u>

## TAKING THE BUS

411. Bus station.    *La gare routière.*    Lah <u>gahr</u> roo-tee-<u>air</u>

412. Intercity bus.    *Le car.*    Luh <u>kar</u>

413. I would like a schedule, please.
     *Je voudrais un horaire, s'il vous plaît.*
     Zhuh voo-<u>dray</u> uhn ore-<u>rair</u> see voo <u>play</u>

414. Local bus.    *Le bus.*    Luh <u>boos</u>

415. Bus stop.    *L'arrêt de bus.*    Lah-<u>ray</u> duh <u>boos</u>

416. A book of tickets, please.
     *Un carnet de tickets, s'il vous plaît.*
     Uhn kar-<u>nay</u> duh tee-<u>kay</u> see voo <u>play</u>

417. Is there a bus that goes to . . . ?
     *Est-ce qu'il y a un bus pour . . . ?*
     Ess keel <u>yah</u> uhn <u>boos</u> poor

418. Which route is it?    *C'est quelle ligne?*    Say kell <u>lee</u>-nyuh

419. Where do I get the bus to go to . . . ?
     *Où est-ce que je prends le bus pour aller à . . . ?*
     Oo ess kuh zhuh <u>prehn</u> luh <u>boos</u> poor ah-<u>lay</u> ah

420. What time is the first bus?
     *C'est à quelle heure le premier bus?*
     Say ah <u>kell</u> er luh <u>pruh</u>-mee-yay <u>boos</u>

421.   When does the last bus leave?
       *C'est à quelle heure le dernier bus?*
       **Say ah <u>kell</u> er luh <u>dare</u>-nyay <u>boos</u>**

422.   Where is the nearest bus stop?
       *Où est l'arrêt de bus le plus proche?*
       **Oo ay lah-<u>ray</u> duh <u>boos</u> luh ploo <u>proh-sh</u>**

423.   Does this bus stop downtown?
       *Est-ce que ce bus s'arrête au centre-ville?*
       **Ess kuh suh <u>boos</u> sah-<u>ret</u> oh sehn-truh <u>veel</u>**

424.   Can you please tell me where to get off?
       *Pourriez-vous me dire où je dois descendre?*
       **Poo-ree-ay voo <u>muh</u> deer oo zhuh <u>dwah</u> duh-<u>san</u>-druh**

425.   The next stop, please.    *Le prochain arrêt, s'il vous plaît.*
       **Luh proh-<u>shihn</u> ah-<u>ray</u> see voo <u>play</u>**

426.   Will I need to change busses?
       *Est-ce que j'aurai besoin de changer de bus?*
       **Ess kuh zhohre-<u>ay</u> <u>buh</u>-zwehn duh shehn-<u>zhay</u> duh <u>boos</u>**

# TAXI!

427.   Taxi stand.    *L'arrêt de taxi.*    **Lah-<u>ray</u> duh tack-<u>see</u>**

428.   Where can I get a taxi?
       *Où est-ce que je peux trouver un taxi?*
       **Oo ess kuh zhuh <u>puh</u> troo-vay uhn tack-<u>see</u>**

429.   Can you please call a taxi?
       *Pourriez-vous m'appeler un taxi?*
       **Poo-ree-ay voo <u>map</u>-lay uhn tack-<u>see</u>**

430.   Would you like to share a taxi?
       *Voudriez-vous partager un taxi?*
       **Voo-dree-ay voo par-tah-<u>zhay</u> uhn tack-<u>see</u>**

431.   How much is the fare into town?
       *C'est combien pour aller en ville?*
       **Say kum-<u>byehn</u> poor ah-lay ehn <u>veel</u>**

432. I'd like to go to . . .    *Je voudrais aller . . .*
     **Zhuh voo-<u>dray</u> ah-<u>lay</u>**

     . . . the airport.    *. . . à l'aéroport.*    **ah lair-oh-<u>pore</u>**

     . . . the train station.    *. . . à la gare.*    **ah lah <u>gahr</u>**

     . . . the bus station.    *. . . à la gare routière.*
     **ah lah <u>gahr</u> roo-tee-<u>air</u>**

433. I'm in a hurry.    *Je suis pressé(e).*    **Zhuh swee press-<u>say</u>**

434. Is it far?    *C'est loin?*    **Say <u>lwehn</u>**

435. Here's the address.    *Voici l'adresse.*    **Vwa-<u>see</u> lah-<u>dress</u>**

436. Can you stop here, please?
     *Pouvez-vous arrêter ici, s'il vous plaît?*
     **Poo-vay-voo ah-ret-<u>ay</u> ee-<u>see</u> see voo <u>play</u>**

437. That's more than what's on the meter.
     *C'est plus qui est sur le compteur.*
     **Say <u>ploos</u> kee <u>ay</u> serr luh comp-<u>terr</u>**

438. I don't have any smaller bills.
     *Désolé, je n'ai pas de plus petits billets.*
     **Day-zoh-<u>lay</u> zhuh nay <u>pah</u> duh ploo puh-<u>tee</u> bee-<u>yay</u>**

439. Keep the change.    *Gardez la monnaie.*
     **Gar-<u>day</u> lah muh-<u>nay</u>**

# TAKING THE SUBWAY

440. Subway.    *Le métro.*    **Luh <u>may</u>-troh**

441. A subway ticket.    *Un ticket.*    **Uhn tee-<u>kay</u>**

442. Where is the closest subway station?
     *Où est la station de métro la plus proche?*
     **Oo ay lah stah-<u>see-yion</u> duh may-<u>troh</u> lah ploo <u>proh-sh</u>**

443. Where is the subway map?    *Où est le plan du métro?*
     **Oo ay luh <u>plehn</u> doo may-<u>troh</u>**

444. Which line do I take to go to . . . ?
     *Quelle ligne de métro est-ce que je prends pour aller à . . . ?*
     **Kell <u>lee</u>-nyuh duh may-<u>troh</u> ess kuh zhuh <u>prehn</u> poor ah-<u>lay</u> ah**

445. I'd like a booklet of tickets, please.
     *Un carnet de tickets, s'il vous plaît.*
     **Uhn kar-<u>nay</u> duh tee-<u>kay</u> see voo <u>play</u>**

446. Is this the right direction for Montparnasse?
     *Est-ce la bonne direction pour Montparnasse?*
     **Ess lah <u>bunn</u> dee-rek-<u>syion</u> poor mohn-par-<u>nahs</u>**

447. Can I change at Châtelet station?
     *Est-ce qu'il y a une correspondance à Châtelet?*
     **Ess keel <u>yah</u> oon kore-ress-pehn-<u>dehns</u> ah shat-<u>lay</u>**

448. What is the next stop?    *Quel est le prochain arrêt?*
     **Kell <u>ay</u> luh proh-<u>shihn</u> ah-<u>ray</u>**

# TRAVELING ON TWO WHEELS

449. Bicycle.    *Un vélo.*    **Uhn vay-<u>low</u>**

450. I'm planning on riding my bike this morning.
     *Je vais faire du vélo ce matin.*
     **Zhuh vay <u>fair</u> doo vay-<u>low</u> suh ma-<u>tihn</u>**

451. Do you have a helmet?    *Avez-vous un casque?*
     **Ah-vay-<u>voo</u> uhn <u>kask</u>**

452. I'd like to rent a bike.    *J'aimerais louer un vélo.*
     **Zhem-<u>ray</u> loo-<u>ay</u> uhn vay-<u>low</u>**

453. Are there bike paths?    *Y a-t-il des pistes cyclables?*
     **Ee yah <u>teel</u> day <u>pees</u>-tuh see-<u>klah</u>-bluh**

454. Scooter.    *Une moto.*    **Oon mow-<u>tow</u>**

455. I'd like to rent a scooter.    *J'aimerais louer une moto.*
     **Zhem-<u>ray</u> loo-<u>ay</u> oon mow-<u>tow</u>**

# GOING ON FOOT

456. Can I get there on foot?    *Est-ce qu'on peut y aller à pied?*
Ess <u>kohn</u> puht ee ah-<u>lay</u> ah <u>pee-yay</u>

457. It's ten minutes away.    *C'est à dix minutes d'ici.*
Set <u>ah</u> dee mee-<u>noot</u> dee-<u>see</u>

458. Do you have a map of the neighborhood?
*Avez-vous un plan du quartier?*
Ah-vay-voo uhn <u>plehn</u> doo kar-<u>tee-yay</u>

459. Is there a guided walk that you recommend?
*Y a-t-il des promenades guidées que vous recommandez?*
Ee yah <u>teel</u> day <u>pruhm</u>-nahd ghee-<u>day</u> kuh
voo ruh-kuh-mehn-<u>day</u>

460. Do you have a guide to local walks?
*Avez-vous un guide des promenades?*
Ah-vay-voo uhn <u>geed</u> day <u>pruhm</u>-nahd

461. How long will this walk take?
*Ça prendra combien de temps?*
Sah prehn-<u>drah</u> kum-<u>byehn</u> duh <u>tehn</u>

462. We'd like to take a hike.
*On voudrait faire une promenade/randonnée.*
Ohn voo-<u>dray</u> fair oon pruhm-<u>nahd</u> / rehn-doh-<u>nay</u>

463. We'd like to go climbing.    *On voudrait faire de l'escalade.*
Ohn voo-<u>dray</u> fair duh <u>less</u>-kah-<u>lahd</u>

464. Do I need walking shoes?
*Est-ce que j'aurai besoin de chaussures de marche?*
Ess <u>kuh</u> zhohre-ay <u>buh</u>-zwehn duh shoh-<u>ser</u> duh <u>marsh</u>

465. Where are the hiking trails?
*Où sont les sentiers de randonnées pédestres?*
Oo sehn lay <u>sehn</u>-tee-yay duh rehn-doh-<u>nay</u> ped-<u>estre</u>

466. Is it a difficult climb?    *Est-ce que ça monte dur?*
Ess <u>kuh</u> sah mehnt <u>door</u>

467.    Is it steep?    *Est-ce que c'est une pente raide?*
Ess <u>kuh</u> sate oon pehnt <u>red</u>

## AT THE HOTEL

468.    Can you suggest a good hotel?
*Pourriez-vous suggérer un bon hôtel?*
Poor-ee-yay <u>voo</u> <u>soog</u>-zhay-<u>ray</u> uhn bohn oh-<u>tell</u>

469.    Can you suggest an inexpensive hotel?
*Pourriez-vous suggérer un bon hôtel pas cher?*
Poor-ee-yay <u>voo</u> <u>soog</u>-zhay-<u>ray</u> uhn bohn oh-<u>tell</u> pah <u>share</u>

470.    Do you have a vacancy?    *Avez-vous une chambre?*
Ah-vay <u>voo</u> oon <u>shahm</u>-bruh

471.    I'd like a double room.
*Je voudrais une chambre pour deux personnes.*
Zhuh voo-<u>dray</u> oon <u>shahm</u>-bruh poor <u>duh</u> pair-<u>sun</u>

472.    I'd like a room for one person.
*Je voudrais une chambre pour une personne.*
Zhuh voo-<u>dray</u> oon <u>shahm</u>-bruh poor <u>oon</u> pair-<u>sun</u>

473.    I'd like a room with two beds.
*Je voudrais une chambre avec deux lits.*
Zhuh voo-<u>dray</u> oon <u>shahm</u>-bruh ah-<u>vek</u> duh <u>lee</u>

474.    I have a reservation under the name "Jones."
*J'ai une réservation au nom de "Jones."*
Zhay oon <u>ray</u>-zair-vah-<u>syion</u> oh nohm duh <u>Jones</u>

475.    Where can I park the car?
*Où est-ce que je peux garer la voiture?*
Oo ess <u>kuh</u> zhuh puh <u>gah</u>-ray lah vwah-<u>toor</u>

476.    For two nights.    *Pour deux nuits.*    Poor <u>duh</u> nwee

477.    May I see the room?    *Je peux voir la chambre?*
Zhuh puh <u>vwahr</u> lah <u>shahm</u>-bruh

478.    Would it be possible to have another room?
*Est-ce que ce serait possible d'avoir une autre chambre?*
Ess kuh suh <u>sray</u> poh-<u>see</u>-bluh dahv-wahr oon <u>oht-ruh</u>
<u>shahm</u>-bruh

479.   Is breakfast included?   *Le petit-déjeuner est compris?*
Luh <u>puh</u>-tee <u>day</u>-zhuhn-ay ay khum-<u>pree</u>

480.   Does the room have . . . ?   *Est-ce que la chambre a . . . ?*
Ess <u>kuh</u> lah <u>shahm</u>-bruh ah

. . . a shower?   . . . *une douche?*   oon <u>doosh</u>

. . . a bath?   . . . *une baignoire?*   oon ben-<u>whahr</u>

. . . a TV?   . . . *une télé?*   oon tay-<u>lay</u>

. . . a high-speed Internet connection?
. . . *une connexion Internet haut-débit?*
oon kuhn-eck-<u>syion</u> ihn-tair-<u>net</u> oh day-<u>bee</u>

. . . air conditioning?   . . . *la climatisation?*
lah <u>kleem</u>-ah-tee-zah-<u>syion</u>

481.   May I have the key?   *Je peux avoir la clé?*
Zhuh puh ahv-<u>wahr</u> lah <u>clay</u>

482.   We'll be back after midnight.
*On sera de retour après minuit.*
Ohn <u>suh</u>-rah duh ruh-toor ah-<u>pray</u> mee-<u>nwee</u>

483.   Will the door be locked?   *La porte sera fermée?*
Lah port <u>suh</u>-rah fair-<u>may</u>

484.   Will we need to ring the bell?   *On aura besoin de sonner?*
Ohn ore-<u>rah</u> <u>buh</u>-zwehn duh sun-<u>nay</u>

# Chapter 3
## Mealtimes

How people talk about mealtimes differs among Francophone countries. In France, *les repas* (meals) consist of *le petit-déjeuner* (breakfast), *le déjeuner* (lunch), and *le dîner* (dinner), whereas in Québec *le déjeuner* (breakfast), *le dîner* (lunch), and *le souper* (dinner) are the principal meals of the day. Children in both countries will come home to *un goûter* (after-school snack), and, if as a traveler you find yourself feeling a bit hungry, by all means stop for *un casse-croûte* (a snack)!

## TALKING ABOUT MEALTIMES AND EATING: GENERAL EXPRESSIONS

485. Breakfast.    *Le petit-déjeuner.*    **Luh <u>puh</u>-tee <u>day</u>-zhuh-<u>nay</u>**

486. Lunch.    *Le déjeuner.*    **Luh <u>day</u>-zhuh-<u>nay</u>**

487. Dinner.    *Le dîner.*    **Luh <u>dee</u>-nay**

488. I'm (very) hungry.    *J'ai (très) faim.*    **Zhay (<u>tray</u>) <u>fihm</u>**

489. I'm not (very) hungry.    *Je n'ai pas (très) faim.*
**Zhuh nay <u>pah</u> (tray) <u>fihm</u>**

490. We're dying of hunger!    *On crève de faim!*
**Ohn <u>krev</u> duh <u>fihm</u>**

491. Would you like more . . . ?    *Vous voulez encore . . . ?*
**Voo voo-<u>lay</u> ehn-<u>kore</u>**

| | | |
|---|---|---|
| . . . salad. | . . . *de la salade.* | **duh lah sah-<u>lahd</u>** |
| . . . chicken. | . . . *du poulet.* | **doo poo-<u>lay</u>** |
| . . . wine. | . . . *du vin.* | **doo vihn** |

492. No thanks, I'm full.    *Non, merci. Je n'ai plus faim.*
**Noh mare-<u>see</u>. Zhuh nay <u>ploo</u> fihm**

493. Yes, just a little, thanks.    *Oui, juste un peu, merci.*
**Wee, <u>zhoost</u> uhn <u>puh</u> mare-<u>see</u>**

494. Enjoy your meal!    *Bon appétit!*    **Bohn <u>ah</u>-pay-<u>tee</u>**

495. It's delicious.    *C'est délicieux.*    **Say <u>day</u>-lee-<u>syuh</u>**

496. Cheers! (formal)    *À la vôtre! (formal)*    **Ah lah <u>vot</u>-ruh**

497. Cheers! (informal)    *À la tienne! (informal)*    **Ah lah <u>tyen</u>**

498. I'm vegetarian.    *Je suis végétarien(ne).*
**Zhuh swee <u>vay</u>-zhay-tahr-ee-<u>ehn</u> / <u>vay</u>-zhay-tahr-ee-<u>yen</u>**

499. I'm vegan.    *Je suis végétalien(ne).*
**Zhuh swee <u>vay</u>-zhay-tahl-ee-<u>ehn</u> / <u>vay</u>-zhay-tahl-ee-<u>yen</u>**

500. A food allergy.    *Une allergie alimentaire.*
**Oon <u>ahl</u>-air-zhee ah-lee-mehn-<u>tair</u>**

501. I'm allergic . . .    *Je suis allergique . . .*
**Zhuh swee <u>zahl</u>-air-<u>zheek</u>**

502. . . . to peanut products.    *. . . aux arachides.*
**oh <u>zahr</u>-ah-<u>sheed</u>**

503. . . . to seafood.    *. . . aux fruits de mer.*
**oh <u>fwee</u> duh <u>mare</u>**

504. I'm lactose intolerant.    *J'ai une intolérance au lactose.*
**Zhay oon <u>ihn</u>-tow-lay-<u>rehns</u> ow lak-<u>tohs</u>**

505. I'm on a diet.    *Je suis un régime.*
**Zhuh <u>swee</u> uhn ray-<u>zheem</u>**

## DINING OUT

506. Can you suggest . . . ?    *Pouvez-vous suggérer . . . ?*
**Poo-vay voo <u>soog</u>-zhay-<u>ray</u>**

507. . . . a good restaurant.    *. . . un bon restaurant.*
**uhn <u>bohn</u> ress-toh-<u>rehn</u>**

508. . . . something close by. . . . *quelque chose près d'ici.*
kell kuh <u>shows</u> <u>pray</u> dee-<u>see</u>

509. . . . a cheap restaurant. . . . *un restaurant pas cher.*
uhn ress-toh-<u>rehn</u> pah <u>share</u>

510. I like . . . cuisine. *J'aime bien la cuisine . . .*
Zhem <u>byehn</u> lah kwee-<u>zeen</u>

| | | |
|---|---|---|
| French. | *française.* | frehn-<u>say</u> |
| Regional. | *régional.* | <u>ray</u>-zhee-on-<u>nahl</u> |
| Italian. | *italienne.* | ee-tahl-<u>yen</u> |
| Spanish. | *espagnole.* | ess-pah-<u>nyole</u> |
| Moroccan. | *marocaine.* | mah-roh-<u>ken</u> |
| Indian. | *indienne.* | ehn-<u>dyen</u> |
| vegetarian. | *végétarienne.* | vay-zhay-tahr-ee-<u>yen</u> |

511. On cherche . . . We're looking for . . . Ohn <u>share</u>-<u>sh</u>

| | | |
|---|---|---|
| . . . a café. | . . . *un café.* | uhn kah-<u>fay</u> |
| . . . a snack bar. | . . . *une buvette.* | oon <u>boo</u>-vet |
| . . . a bar. | . . . *un bar.* | uhn <u>bar</u> |
| . . . a restaurant. | . . . *un restaurant.* | uhn ress-toh-<u>rehn</u> |
| . . . a crêpe place. | . . . *une crêperie.* | oon krep-<u>ree</u> |
| . . . a bistro. | . . . *un bistro.* | uhn <u>bee</u>-stroh |
| . . . a tea room. | . . . *un salon de thé.* | uhn sah-<u>lohn</u> duh <u>tay</u> |
| . . . a deli. | . . . *un traiteur.* | uhn tret-<u>ter</u> |

512. I'd like to reserve a table . . .
*Je voudrais réserver une table . . .*
Zhuh voo-<u>dray</u> ray-zair-<u>vay</u> oon-<u>tab</u>-luh

. . . for two. . . . *pour deux.* poor <u>duh</u>

. . . for tonight. . . . *pour ce soir.* poor suh <u>swahr</u>

. . . for tomorrow night. . . . *pour demain soir.*
poor <u>duh</u>-mihn <u>swahr</u>

513. May I see the menu, please?
*Je peux voir la carte, s'il vous plaît?*
Zhuh puh <u>vwahr</u> lah <u>kart</u> see voo <u>play</u>

514. What do you recommend . . . ?
*Qu'est-ce que vous recommandez . . . ?*
**Kess kuh voo ruh-koh-mehn-day**

     . . . as an appetizer.     . . . *comme hors d'œuvre.*
**kuhm ore-duhv-ruh**

     . . . as a main course.     . . . *comme plat principal.*
**kuhm plah prihn-see-pahl**

     . . . as a cheese.     . . . *comme fromage.*    **kuhm fro-mah-zh**

     . . . as a dessert.     . . . *comme dessert.*    **kuhm deh-sare**

515. I'll have . . .    *Je prends . . .*    **Zhuh prehn**

     . . . the tourist menu.     . . . *le menu touristique.*
**luh muh-noo too-rees-teek**

     . . . the fixed-priced menu.     . . . *le menu à prix fixe.*
**luh muh-noo ah pree feex**

     . . . all-taxes-included price.     . . . *la formule TTC.*
**lah fore-mool tay-tay-say**

516. Enjoy your meal!    *Bon appétit!*    **Bohn ah-pay-tee**

517. Thanks, same to you!    *Merci, à vous aussi!*
**Mare-see ah voo zoh-see**

518. It's . . .    *C'est . . .*    **Say**

     salty.     *salé.*     **sah-lay**

     spicy.     *épicé.*     **ay-pee-say**

519. It's not . . . enough.    *Ce n'est pas assez . . .*
**Suh nay pah ah-say**

     sweet.     *sucré.*     **soo-kray**

     hot.     *pimenté.*     **pee-mehn-tay**

520. It's too . . .    *C'est trop . . .*    **Say troh**

     sour.     *aigre/acide.*     **egg-ruh / ah-seed**

     bitter.     *amer.*     **ah-mare**

521. It's a bit tasteless.    *C'est un peu fade.*    **Set uhn puh fahd**

522. More . . . please.    *Encore . . . s'il vous plaît.*
Ehn-<u>kore</u> . . . see voo <u>play</u>

bread.        . . . *du pain*        doo <u>pihn</u>

water.        . . . *de l'eau.*        duh <u>loh</u>

523. The bill, please.    *L'addition, s'il vous plaît.*
Lah-dee-<u>syion</u> see voo <u>play</u>

524. Is the tip included?    *Le service est compris?*
Luh sehr-<u>vees</u> ay kuhm-<u>pree</u>

## MENU: GENERAL ITEMS

525. Bread.    *Le pain.*    Luh <u>pihn</u>

526. Salt.    *Le sel.*    Luh <u>sell</u>

527. Pepper.    *Le poivre.*    Luh <u>pwahv</u>-ruh

528. Butter.    *Le beurre.*    Luh <u>buhr</u>

529. Sugar.    *Le sucre.*    Luh <u>sook</u>-ruh

530. Vinaigrette dressing.    *La sauce vinaigrette.*
Lah <u>sohse</u> vee-neh-<u>gret</u>

531. Tap water.    *L'eau du robinet.*    Loh duh <u>roh</u>-bee-nay

532. Mineral water (flat).    *L'eau plate.*    Loh <u>plaht</u>

533. Sparkling water.    *L'eau pétillante.*    Loh <u>pay</u>-tee-<u>yehnt</u>

534. with ice.    *avec des glaçons.*    ah-<u>vek</u> day <u>glah</u>-sohn

535. Mustard.    *La moutarde.*    Lah moo-<u>tard</u>

536. Garlic.    *L'ail.*    <u>Ly</u>-yuh

## BREAKFAST

In France, breakfast tends to be a light meal, sometimes consisting of bread or a pastry and coffee. Note that if you're looking for that large cup of coffee so prevalent in the United States, you'll want to order *un café américain*—espresso diluted with hot water—as ordering *un café* will get you an espresso. Breakfast in Québec tends to have more in common with the hearty American breakfast.

537. I'll have . . .    *Je prends . . .*    **Zhuh prehn**
     a coffee.    *un café.*    **uhn kah-fay**
     a regular coffee.    *un café américain.*
     **uhn kah-fay ah-mary-kihn**
     a decaf.    *un déca.*    **uhn day-kah**

538. We'd like . . .    *On aimerait . . .*    **Ohn ehm-ray**
     coffee with milk.    *un café au lait.*    **uhn kah-fay oh lay**
     a large coffee with frothy milk.    *un grand crème.*
     **uhn grehn krem**

539. In the mornings I have . . .    *Le matin je prends . . .*
     **Luh mah-tihn zhuh prehn**
     Tea . . .    *un thé . . .*    **uhn tay**
     . . . with lemon.    *. . . au citron.*    **oh see-trohn**
     . . . with milk.    *. . . au lait.*    **oh lay**

540. Do you want . . . ?
     *Voulez-vous . . . ? (formal)    Tu veux . . . ? (informal)*
     **Voo-lay voo    Too vuh**
     Hot chocolate.    *Un chocolat chaud.*
     **Uhn show-koh-lah show**

541. I would rather have . . .    *J'aimerais plutôt avoir . . .*
     **Zhem-ray ploo-tow ahv-wahr**
     A glass of fruit juice.    *Un jus de fruits.*
     **Uhn zhoo duh fwee**
     A glass of orange juice.    *Un jus d'orange.*
     **Uhn zhoo dow-rehnzh**

542. I would like . . .    *Je voudrais . . .*    **Zhuh voo-dray . . .**
     . . . some toast.    *. . . du pain grille.*    **doo pihn gree-yay**
     with jam.    *avec de la confiture.*
     **ah-vek duh lah kehn-fee-toor**
     with honey.    *avec du miel.*    **ah-vek doo myel**

... some cereal.   ... *des céréales.*
day **say-ree-yahl**

... an egg.   ... *un œuf.*   uh **nuf**

... some fried eggs.   ... *des œufs au plat.*
day **zuh** oh **plah**

... an omelet.   ... *une omelette.*   oon uhm-**let**

... a soft-boiled egg.   ... *un œuf à la coque.*
uh **nuf** ah lah **kuk**

... a cheese omelet.   ... *une omelette au fromage.*
oon uhm-**let** oh fro-**mah-zh**

... bacon and eggs.   ... *des œufs avec du lard.*
day **zuh** ah-vek doo **lahr**

... ham and eggs.   ... *des œufs au jambon.*
day **zuh** oh zhahm-**bohn**

... a yogurt.   ... *un yaourt.*   uhn yah-**oort**

... breakfast pastries.   ... *des viennoiseries.*
day **vyen-wahz-uhr-ree**

... a croissant.   ... *un croissant.*   uhn **kwah**-sehn

... a chocolate-filled croissant.   ... *un pain au chocolat.*
uhn **pihn** oh **show-koh-lah**

... a raisin bun.   ... *un pain au raisin.*
uhn **pihn** oh ray-**zihn**


## APPETIZERS, LUNCH ITEMS, AND SALAD

543.   We'd like to have a light meal.
*On a envie de prendre un repas léger.*
Ohn ah ehn-**vee** duh **prehn**-druh uhn ruh-**pah** lay-**zhay**

544.   Soup.   *La soupe.*   Lah **soop**

545.   Chicken soup.   *La soupe au poulet.*   Lah **soop** oh **poo**-lay

546.   Vegetable soup.   *Le potage / la soupe aux légumes.*
Luh pow-**tahzh** / lah **soop** oh **lay**-goom

547.   French onion soup.   *La soupe à l'oignon gratinée.*
Lah **soop** ah luh-**nyion** grah-tee-**nay**

548. Fish soup.    *La bouillabaisse.*    Lah <u>boo</u>-yah-<u>bess</u>

549. Plate of cold meat.    *Une assiette anglaise.*
Oon ahs-<u>yet</u> ehn-<u>glez</u>

550. I feel like having . . .    *J'ai envie de prendre* . . .
Zhay ehn-<u>vee</u> duh <u>prehn</u>-druh

   a sandwich.    *un sandwich.*    uhn sehnd-<u>weech</u>

   a ham sandwich.    *un sandwich au jambon.*
   uhn sehnd-<u>weech</u> oh zhahm-<u>bohn</u>

   a tuna sandwich.    *un sandwich au thon.*
   uhn sehnd-<u>weech</u> oh <u>tohn</u>

   a cheese sandwich.    *un sandwich au fromage.*
   uhn sehnd-<u>weech</u> oh fro-<u>mah-zh</u>

551. He / She will have . . .    *Il / elle prend* . . .
Eel / el <u>prehn</u>

   some quiche.    *de la quiche.*    duh lah <u>keesh</u>

   a green salad.    *une salade verte.*    oon sah-<u>lahd</u> <u>vair</u>-tuh

   a tomato salad.    *une salade de tomates.*
   oon sah-<u>lahd</u> duh tow-<u>maht</u>

   eggs with mayonnaise.    *des œufs mayonnaise.*
   day <u>zuh</u> my-yo-<u>nez</u>

# MAIN COURSE

552. We'd like to eat . . .    *On aimerait manger* . . .
Ohn em-<u>ray</u> mahn-<u>zhay</u>

   . . . now.    . . . *maintenant.*    <u>mihn</u>-tuh-nehn

   . . . later.    . . . *plus tard.*    ploo <u>tar</u>

553. I'm ordering . . .    *Je commande* . . .    Zhuh kuh-<u>mehnd</u>
   some roast chicken.    *du poulet rôti.*    doo <u>poo</u>-lay row-<u>tee</u>
   some grilled fish.    *du poisson grillé.*
   doo <u>pwah</u>-suhn <u>gree</u>-yay
   some salmon.    *du saumon.*    doo soh-<u>mohn</u>

554. I like . . .    *J'aime bien* . . .    Zhem <u>byehn</u>
   seafood.    *les fruits de mer.*    lay <u>fwee</u> duh <u>mare</u>

| | | |
|---|---|---|
| mussels. | *les moules.* | lay <u>mool</u> |
| crab. | *le crabe.* | luh <u>krahb</u> |
| shrimp. | *les crevettes.* | lay kruh-<u>vet</u> |
| lobster. | *le homard.* | luh <u>oh</u>-mar |
| oysters. | *les huîtres.* | lay <u>zweet</u>-ruh |

555. I'm not too fond of . . .    *Je n'aime pas beaucoup . . .*
Zhuh <u>nem</u> pah <u>boh</u>-koo

| | | |
|---|---|---|
| steak. | *le bifteck.* | luh beef-<u>tek</u> |
| leg of lamb. | *le gigot d'agneau.* | luh zhee-<u>go</u> dehn-<u>yoh</u> |
| pork. | *le porc.* | luh <u>pore</u> |
| ham. | *le jambon* | luh zhahm-<u>bohn</u> |

556. I rarely eat . . .    *Je mange rarement . . .*
Zhuh <u>mehnzh</u> rahr-<u>mehn</u>

| | | |
|---|---|---|
| veal. | *du veau.* | doo <u>voh</u> |
| roast beef. | *du rosbif.* | doo <u>rohz</u>-beef |

A filet of turkey.    *Une escalope de dinde.*
oon ess-kah-<u>lope</u> duh <u>dihn</u>-duh

557. Pasta.    *Les pâtes.*    Lay <u>paht</u>

558. Choice of vegetable.    *Légume au choix.*
Lay-<u>goom</u> oh <u>shwah</u>

559. A vegetarian couscous.    *Un couscous aux legumes.*
Uhn <u>koos</u>-koos oh lay-<u>goom</u>

560. Stew.    *Le ragout.*    Luh <u>rah</u>-goo

561. Rice.    *Le riz.*    Luh <u>ree</u>

# FRUITS AND VEGETABLES

562. If I'm a little hungry, I eat . . .
*Si j'ai un peu faim je mange . . .*
See zhay uhn <u>puh</u> fehm zhuh <u>mehnzh</u>

An apple.    *Une pomme.*    oon <u>pum</u>

An orange.    *Une orange.*    oon oh-<u>rehn</u>-zh

A grapefruit.    *Le pamplemousse.*    luh <u>pahmp</u>-luh-moos

563.  Can I give you . . . ?
*Je peux vous donner . . . ? (formal)*
*Je peux te donner . . . ? (informal)*
Zhuh <u>puh</u> voo <u>dunn</u>-nay    Zhuh <u>puh</u> tuh <u>dunn</u>-nay

some bananas.    *des bananas.*    day bah-<u>nehn</u>

some grapes.    *du raisin.*    doo <u>ray</u>-zihn

564.  I need . . .    *J'ai besoin . . .*    Zhay <u>buh</u>-zhwehn

a lemon.    *d'un citron.*    duhn <u>see</u>-trohn

a lime.    *d'un citron vert.*    duhn <u>see</u>-trohn <u>vair</u>

a peach.    *d'une pêche.*    doon <u>pesh</u>

565.  A fruit salad.    *une salade de fruits.*
oon sah-<u>lahd</u> duh <u>fwee</u>

566.  a green salad.    *une salade verte.*
oon sah-<u>lahd</u> <u>vair</u>-tuh

567.  I'd like to buy . . .    *J'aimerais acheter . . .*
Zhem-<u>ray</u> ahsh-<u>tay</u> . . .

some carrots.    *des carottes.*    day kah-<u>rut</u>

some potatoes.    *des pommes de terre.*    day <u>pum</u> duh <u>tair</u>

some tomatoes.    *des tomates.*    day tow-<u>maht</u>

some lettuce.    *de la laitue.*    duh lah <u>lay</u>-too

an eggplant.    *une aubergine.*    oon <u>oh</u>-bair-<u>zheen</u>

some zucchini.    *des courgettes.*    day <u>koor</u>-zhet

some parsley.    *du persil.*    doo <u>pair</u>-see

some cauliflower.    *du chou-fleur.*    doo <u>shoo</u>-fler

568.  To make a salad, I'll need to buy . . .
*Pour faire une salade, j'aurai besoin d'acheter . . .*
Poor fair oon sah-<u>lahd</u> zhohre-ay <u>buh</u>-zwehn dahsh-<u>tay</u>

some green peppers.    *des poivrons.*    day <u>pwah</u>-vrohn

some mushrooms.    *des champignons.*
day <u>shahm</u>-pee-<u>nyion</u>

some spinach.    *des épinards.*    **day <u>zay</u>-pee-<u>nar</u>**

some cucumbers.    *des concombres.*    **day kuhn-<u>khum</u>-bruh**

some leeks.    *des poireaux.*    **day <u>pwah</u>-roh**

## DESSERT

In France, a cheese course frequently is served either before dessert or in place of it. Putting together a good cheese plate or *plateau de fromages* is an art in itself, as the cheeses should represent a harmonious variety of texture, milk type, color, and regional origin.

569.    What would like for dessert?
*Qu'est-ce que vous prenez comme dessert?*
**Kess kuh voo <u>pruh</u>-nay kuhm duh-<u>sair</u>**

570.    What desserts do you have?
*Qu'est-ce que vous avez comme dessert?*
**Kess kuh voo <u>zah</u>-vay kuhm duh-<u>sair</u>**

571.    May I see the cheese plate?
*Puis-je voir le plateau de fromages?*
**Pwee-zhuh <u>vwahr</u> luh <u>plah</u>-toh duh fro-<u>mah-zh</u>**

572.    Can you suggest . . .    *Pouvez-vous me suggérer . . .*
**Poo-vay-voo <u>muh</u> soog-<u>zhay</u>-ray**

. . . a mild cheese?    . . . *un fromage doux?*
**uhn fro-mah-zh <u>doo</u>**

. . . a blue cheese?    . . . *un fromage bleu?*
**uhn fro-mah-zh <u>bluh</u>**

. . . a good regional cheese?    . . . *un bon fromage régional?*
**uhn <u>bohn</u> fro-mah-zh <u>ray</u>-zhee-on-<u>nahl</u>**

. . . a goat cheese?    . . . *un chèvre?*    **uhn <u>shev</u>-ruh**

573.    We would like a plate of different types of cheese.
*On voudrait un plat de fromages assortis.*
**Ohn voo-<u>dray</u> uhn <u>plah</u> duh fro-<u>mah-zh</u> ah-sore-<u>tee</u>**

574.    Some chocolate cake.    *Du gâteau au chocolat.*
**Doo gah-<u>toh</u> oh <u>show</u>-koh-lah**

575.    Some ice cream.    *De la glace.*    **Duh lah <u>glahss</u>**

576. Some vanilla ice cream.    *De la glace à la vanille.*
**Duh lah <u>glahss</u> ah lah <u>vah</u>-nee**

577. Some apple pie.    *De la tarte aux pommes.*
**Duh lah <u>tart</u> oh <u>pum</u>**

578. Some chocolate mousse.    *De la mousse au chocolat.*
**Duh lah <u>moos</u> oh <u>show</u>-koh-<u>lah</u>**

## BEVERAGES

579. Would you like to have a drink?
*Vous voulez boire quelque chose?*
**Voo voo-lay <u>bwahr</u> kel-kuh <u>shows</u>**

580. What will you have?    *Qu'est-ce que vous prenez?*
**Kess kuh voo <u>pruh</u>-nay**

581. I'm buying!    *C'est moi qui paie!*    **Say <u>mwah</u> kee <u>pay</u>**

582. I'm buying this round of drinks.
*Je vous offre cette tournée.*    **Zhu vooz <u>uhf-ruh</u> set toor-<u>nay</u>**

583. The wine list, please.    *La carte des vins, s'il vous plaît.*
**Lah kart day <u>vihn</u> see voo <u>play</u>**

584. A pitcher of water.    *Une carafe d'eau.*    **Oon <u>kah</u>-rahf <u>doh</u>**

585. A bottle of mineral water.    *Une bouteille d'eau minérale.*
**Oon boo-tay <u>doh</u> meen-ay-<u>rahl</u>**

586. Some lemonade.    *De la citronnade.*
**Duh lah <u>see</u>-troh-<u>nahd</u>**

587. A fruit juice.    *Un jus de fruit.*    **Uhn <u>zhoo</u> duh <u>fwee</u>**

588. Some cider.    *Du cidre.*    **Doo <u>see</u>-druh**

589. A glass of milk.    *Un verre de lait.*    **Uhn <u>vair</u> duh <u>lay</u>**

590. Some iced tea.    *Du thé glacé.*    **Doo <u>tay</u> glah-<u>say</u>**

591. A bottle of red wine.    *Une bouteille de vin rouge.*
**Oon boo-<u>tay</u> duh <u>vihn</u> roozh**

592.  Un pitcher of rosé.    *Un pichet de vin rosé.*
      **Uhn pee-<u>shay</u> duh <u>vihn</u>-roh-zay**

593.  A bottle of white wine.    *Une bouteille de vin blanc.*
      **Oon boo-<u>tay</u> duh <u>vihn</u> blehn**

594.  A beer.    *Une bière.*    **Oon <u>bee</u>-yair**

595.  What draft beers do you have?
      *Qu'est-ce que vous avez comme bière pression?*
      **Kess kuh voo <u>zah</u>-vay kuhm <u>bee</u>-yair press-<u>yion</u>**

596.  I'd like to try . . .    *J'aimerais essayer . . .*
      **Zhem-<u>ray</u> ess-ay-<u>yay</u>**

      . . . a local beer.    . . . *une bière de la région.*
      **oon <u>bee</u>-yair duh lah-<u>rayzh</u>-yion**

      . . . a stout beer.    . . . *une bière noire.*    **oon <u>bee</u>-yair <u>nwahr</u>**

      . . . a lager.    . . . *une bière blonde.*    **oon <u>bee</u>-yair blone-<u>duh</u>**

      . . . a brown ale.    . . . *une bière rousse.*    **oon <u>bee</u>-yair <u>roos</u>**

      . . . a dark beer.    . . . *une bière brune.*    **oon <u>bee</u>-yair <u>broon</u>**

597.  What do you recommend?    *Qu'est-ce que vous conseillez?*
      **Kess kuh voo <u>kon</u>-say-<u>yay</u>**

598.  Do you have . . .    *Avez-vous une bière . . .*
      **Ah-vay voo oon <u>bee</u>-yair**

      . . . a lighter beer?    . . . *plus légère?*    **<u>ploo</u> lay-<u>zhay</u>**

      . . . a darker beer?    . . . *plus foncée?*    **<u>ploo</u> fon-<u>say</u>**

599.  What's the house cocktail?
      *Quel est le cocktail de la maison?*
      **Kell ay luh <u>cock</u>-tel duh lah <u>may</u>-zuhn**

600.  A whiskey.    *Un whisky.*    **Uhn <u>wee</u>-skee**

601.  A pre-dinner drink    *Un apéritif.*    **Uhn ah-<u>pay</u>-ree-<u>teef</u>**

602.  An after-dinner drink.    *Un digestif.*    **Uhn <u>dee</u>-zhes-<u>teef</u>**

# Chapter 4
## Leisure Activities

## SIGHTSEEING

Most French towns have a local *syndicat d'initiative* or *office du tourisme* (tourist office) that is an excellent resource for travelers. Don't hesitate to pay a visit, as the staff is usually eager to suggest local attractions, recommend interesting excursions, and provide you with helpful maps, brochures, and other useful information that will help you make the most of your time there.

603. Where is the nearest tourist office?
*Où est le syndicat d'initiative le plus proche?*
Oo ay luh sihn-dee-<u>ka</u> dee-nee-sia-<u>teev</u> luh ploo <u>proh-sh</u>

604. What local attractions do you recommend?
*Quels centres d'intérêts est-ce que vous nous conseillez?*
Kell <u>sehn</u>-truh dan-tair-<u>ay</u> ess-kuh voo noo <u>kon</u>-say-<u>yay</u>

605. We're interested in a guided visit.
*On s'intéresse à une visite guidée.*
Ohn sihn-tair-<u>ess</u> ah oon vee-<u>zeet</u> ghee-<u>day</u>

606. What are the hours of operation?
*Quelles sont les heures d'ouverture?*
Kell sohn laze <u>er</u> doo-vair-<u>toor</u>

607. How much is the entrance fee?     *Quel est le prix d'entrée?*
Kell ay luh <u>pree</u> dehn-<u>tray</u>

608. Where can I buy tickets?
*Où est-ce qu'on peut acheter des billets?*
Oo ess kohn puh tah-<u>shtay</u> day bee-<u>yay</u>

609. I'd like two tickets for tonight's show.
*J'aimerais deux places pour ce soir.*
Zhem-<u>ray</u> duh <u>plahss</u> poor suh <u>swahr</u>

610. What time does it start/end?
*Ça commence / finit à quelle heure?*
Sah kuh-<u>mehnse</u> / fee-<u>nee</u> ah <u>kell</u> er

611. Is there a reduced ticket price for . . . ?
*Est-ce qu'il y a un tarif . . . ?*    Ess keel yah uhn tah-<u>reef</u>

. . . seniors.      . . . *troisième âge.*    <u>twah</u>-zyem ahzh

. . . students.    . . . *étudiant.*    ay-too-<u>dyehn</u>

. . . children.    . . . *enfants.*    ehn-<u>fehn</u>

. . . the unemployed.    . . . *chômeurs.*    show-<u>mer</u>

. . . groups.    . . . *groupe.*    <u>groop</u>

612. We'd like to visit . . .    *On aimerait visiter . . .*
Ohn em-<u>ray</u> vee-zee-<u>tay</u>

. . . an art museum.    . . . *un musée d'art.*
uhn moo-<u>zay</u> <u>dar</u>

. . . a cemetery.    . . . *un cimetière.*    uhn see-mee-<u>tyair</u>

. . . the shopping district.    . . . *le quartier commercial.*
luh <u>kar</u>-tee-yay ko-mer-see-<u>ahl</u>

613. We'd like to see . . .    *On aimerait voir . . .*
Ohn em-<u>ray</u> vwahr

. . . a concert.    . . . *un concert.*    uhn kon-<u>sair</u>

. . . a play.    . . . *une pièce de théâtre.*
oon pee-<u>yes</u> duh tay-<u>aht</u>-ruh

. . . a movie.    . . . *un film.*    uhn feem

. . . an exhibit.    . . . *une exposition.*
oon ex-poh-zee-syion

. . . an opera.    . . . *un opéra.*    uhn oh-pay-rah

614. We'd like to go . . .    *On aimerait aller . . .*
On em-<u>ray</u> ah-<u>lay</u>

. . . to a nightclub.    . . . *dans une boîte de nuit.*
dehnz oon <u>bwaht</u> duh <u>nwee</u>

... to a bar.   ... *à un bar.*   ah uhn <u>bahr</u>

... to a movie.   ... *au cinéma.*   oh <u>see</u>-nay-<u>mah</u>

615. My kids and I would like to go ...
*Mes enfants et moi aimerions aller ...*
Maze ehn-<u>fehn</u> ay <u>mwah</u> <u>em</u>-ree-ohn ah-<u>lay</u>

... to the zoo.   ... *au zoo.*   oh <u>zoh</u>

... to a playground.   ... *sur une aire de jeux.*
soor oon <u>air</u> duh <u>zhuh</u>

... to a garden.   ... *à un jardin.*   ah uhn zhar-<u>dihn</u>

... to a pool.   ... *à une piscine.*   ah oon <u>pee</u>-seen

616. Would it be possible ... ?   *Est-ce que ce serait possible ... ?*
Ess kuh <u>suh</u> ser-ay poh-<u>see</u>-bluh

... to go a beach.   ... *d'aller sur une plage.*
<u>dah</u>-lay soor oon <u>plah</u>-zh

... go to a park.   ... *d'aller dans un parc.*
<u>dah</u>-lay dehnz uhn <u>par</u>

... go to a botanical garden.
... *d'aller dans un jardin botanique.*
<u>dah</u>-lay dehnz uhn zhar-<u>dihn</u> boh-tah-<u>neek</u>

... visit a cathedral?   ... *de visiter une cathédrale?*
duh vee-zee-<u>tay</u> oon <u>kah</u>-tay-dral

... to a soccer game?   ... *aller à un match de foot?*
<u>dah</u>-lay ah uhn <u>match</u> duh <u>foot</u>

# INTERESTS AND HOBBIES

617. I'm interested ...   *Je m'intéresse ...*
Zhuh <u>mihn</u>-tair-<u>ess</u>

... in films.   ... *au cinema.*   oh <u>see</u>-nay-mah

... in architecture.   ... *à l'architecture.*
ah <u>lar</u>-shee-tek-toor

... in modern art.   ... *à l'art moderne.*
ah <u>lar</u> mow-<u>dairn</u>

618. I enjoy talking about . . .    *J'aime discuter de . . .*
**Zhem** dee-skoo-<u>tay</u> duh

. . . religion.    . . . *la religion*    lah <u>ruh</u>-lee-zhion

. . . current events.    . . . *l'actualité.*    <u>lak</u>-too-al-ee-<u>tay</u>

. . . economics.    . . . *(des) [de + les] sciences économiques.*
lay see-<u>yehns</u> <u>ay</u>-koh-noh-<u>meek</u>

. . . science.    . . . *la science.*    lah <u>see</u>-yehns

619. Are you interested in politics?
*Vous vous intéressez à la politique?*
**Voo vooz** <u>ihn</u>-tay-ray-<u>say</u> ah lah <u>poh</u>-lee-<u>teek</u>

620. I agree.    *Je suis d'accord.*    **Zhuh swee** <u>dah</u>-kore

621. I totally disagree!    *Je ne suis pas du tout d'accord!*
**Zhuh nuh swee** <u>pah</u> doo too <u>dah</u>-kore

622. I'm studying . . .    *J'étudie . . .*    **Zhay-too-<u>dee</u>**

. . . painting.    . . . *la peinture.*    lah <u>pihn</u>-toor

. . . music.    . . . *la musique.*    lah moo-<u>zeek</u>

. . . fashion.    . . . *la mode.*    lah mode

. . . photography.    . . . *photographie.*    lah <u>pho</u>-to-grah-<u>fee</u>

623. I like . . .    *J'aime . . .*    **Zhem**

. . . sports.    . . . *les sports.*    lay <u>spore</u>

. . . reading.    . . . *la lecture.*    lah lek-<u>toor</u>

. . . knitting.    . . . *faire du tricot.*    fair doo <u>tree</u>-koh

. . . drawing.    . . . *le dessin.*    luh <u>dess</u>-ihn

. . . in sculpture.    . . . *la sculpture.*    lah <u>skoolp</u>-toor

624. I really like . . .    *J'aime bien . . .*    **Zhem** <u>byehn</u>

# SPORTS

625. Is there a place nearby where I can . . . ?
*Est-ce qu'il y a un endroit près d'ici où je peux . . . ?*
**Ess keel yah uhn** <u>uhn</u>-dwah pray dee-<u>see</u> oo zhuh <u>puh</u>

. . . ski.    . . . *faire du ski.*    fair doo <u>skee</u>

. . . play tennis.    . . . *jouer au tennis.*
zhoo-ay oh <u>ten</u>-nees

. . . swim.    . . . *nager.*    <u>nah</u>-zhay

. . . go hiking.    . . . *faire de la randonnée.*
fair duh lah <u>rehn</u>-doh-<u>nay</u>

. . . go camping.    . . . *faire du camping.*
fair doo <u>kahm</u>-ping

. . . mountain climb.    . . . *faire de l'alpinisme.*
fair duh <u>lal</u>-peen-<u>eez</u>-muh

. . . go biking.    . . . *faire du vélo.*    fair doo <u>vay</u>-loh

. . . water ski.    . . . *faire du ski nautique.*
fair doo <u>skee</u> noh-<u>teek</u>

. . . play golf.    . . . *jouer au golf.*    zhoo-ay oh <u>golf</u>

. . . go ice skating.    . . . *patiner.*    <u>pah</u>-teen-<u>ay</u>

# HOUSES OF WORSHIP

626.    I am . . .    *Je suis . . .*    Zhuh swee

. . . Christian.    . . . *chrétien. (m.)*    . . . *chrétienne. (f.)*
<u>kray</u>-tyen / <u>kray</u>-tyen-nuh

. . . Catholic.    . . . *catholique.*    <u>kat</u>-oh-<u>leek</u>

. . . Jewish.    . . . *juif. (m.)*    . . . *juive. (f.)*
zhweef / zhweev

. . . Muslim.    . . . *musulman. (m.)*    . . . *musulmane. (f.)*
<u>moo</u>-zool-mehn / <u>moo</u>-zool-mehn-uh

. . . atheist.    . . . *athée.*    <u>ah</u>-tay

627.    Is there . . . nearby?    *Y a-t-il . . . près d'ici?*
Ee yah <u>teel</u> . . . pray dee-<u>see</u>

a Protestant church.    *un temple protestant.*
uhn <u>tahm</u>-pluh <u>proh</u>-tes-tehn

a Catholic church.    *une église catholique.*
oon ay-<u>gleez</u> <u>kah</u>-toh-<u>leek</u>

a synagogue.    *une synagogue.*    oon <u>seen</u>-oh-gog

a mosque.   *une mosquée.*    oon <u>moss</u>-kay

a religious site.   *un site religieux.*    uhn <u>seet</u> ruh-leezh-<u>yuh</u>

When is the service?   *Quelle est l'heure de l'office?*
kell ay <u>ler</u> duh low-<u>fees</u>

628.   Am I allowed to go inside?   *Est-ce qu'on peut entrer?*
Ess kohn <u>puh</u> ehn-<u>tray</u>

# Chapter 5
## Shopping

## BANKING AND MONEY

629. Is there . . . nearby?  *Est-ce qu'il y a . . . près d'ici?*
Ess keel <u>yah</u> . . . pray dee-<u>see</u>

630. A bank.  *Une banque.*  **Oon <u>behnk</u>**

631. An ATM.  *Un distributeur/guichet automatique.*
Uhn dee-stree-boo-<u>ter</u> / ghee-<u>shay</u> oh-toh-mah-<u>teek</u>

632. An American Express office.  *Un bureau American Express.*
Uhn <u>boo</u>-roh American Express

633. A currency exchange.  *Un bureau de change.*
Uhn <u>boo</u>-roh duh <u>shehnzh</u>

634. I'd like . . .  *Je voudrais . . .*  **Zhuh voo-<u>dray</u>**

. . . to change some money.  *. . . changer de l'argent.*
shehn-zhay duh lar-<u>zhehn</u>

. . . to cash a traveler's check.
*. . . encaisser un chèque de voyage.*
ehn kess-ay uhn <u>shek</u> duh voy-<u>ahzh</u>

. . . to withdraw some money.  *. . . retirer de l'argent.*
<u>ruh</u>-tee-ray duh lar-<u>zhehn</u>

635. May I please have . . . ?  *Est-ce que je peux avoir . . . ?*
Ess kuh zhuh puh ahv-<u>wahr</u>

. . . some change.  *. . . de la monnaie, s'il vous plaît.*
duh lah muh-<u>nay</u> see voo <u>play</u>

. . . smaller bills.    . . . *des billets plus petits, s'il vous plaît.*
**day bee-<u>yay</u> ploo <u>puh</u>-tee see voo <u>play</u>**

636.    He wrote a bad check.    *Il a fait un chèque en bois.*
**Eel ah fay uhn <u>shek</u> ehn <u>bwah</u>**

# SHOPPING

637.    I'd like to do a bit of window shopping.
*J'aimerais faire du lèche-vitrine.*
**Zhem-<u>ray</u> fair doo <u>lesh</u>-vee-<u>treen</u>**

638.    How much does this cost?    *Combien coûte ceci?*
**Kum-<u>byehn</u> koot suh-<u>see</u>**

639.    Where are the cash registers, please?
*Où est la caisse, s'il vous plaît?*    **Oo ay lah <u>kess</u>, see voo <u>play</u>**

640.    I'd like to pay . . .    *J'aimerais régler . . .*
**Zhem-<u>ray</u> reg-<u>lay</u>**

. . . with cash.    . . . *en espèces.*    **ehn ess-<u>spess</u>**

. . . by check.    . . . *par chèque.*    **pahr <u>shek</u>**

. . . by credit card.    . . . *par carte de credit.*
**pahr <u>kart</u> duh cray-<u>dee</u>**

641.    May I have the receipt?    *Est-ce que je peux avoir le reçu?*
**Ess kuh zhuh puh ahv-<u>wahr</u> luh ruh-<u>soo</u>**

642.    Is there . . . nearby?    *Est-ce qu'il y a . . . près d'ici?*
**Ess keel <u>yah</u> . . . pray dee-<u>see</u>**

a department store.    *un grand magasin.*
**uhn <u>grehn</u> mah-gah-<u>zihn</u>**

a clothing store.    *un magasin de vêtements.*
**uhn mah-gah-<u>zihn</u> duh <u>vet</u>-mehn**

a shoe store.    *un magasin de chaussures.*
**uhn mah-gah-<u>zihn</u> duh shoh-<u>ser</u>**

a stationery store.    *une papeterie.*    **oon <u>pah</u>-pet-ree**

a bookstore.    *une librairie.*    **oon <u>lee</u>-brair-ee** a jewelry store.  *une bijouterie.*  oon <u>bee</u>-zhoot-ree

a tobacconist.  *un tabac.*  uhn <u>tah</u>-bah

a bakery.  *une boulangerie.*  oon <u>boo</u>-lehn-zhree

a pastry shop.  *une patisserie.*  oon <u>pah</u>-tee-sree

a convenience store.  *une épicerie.*  oon <u>ay</u>-pee-sree

a supermarket.  *un supermarché.*  uhn <u>soo</u>-per-mar-<u>shay</u>

a deli.  *un traiteur.*  uhn tret-<u>ter</u>

an open-air market.  *un marché en plein air.*
uhn mar-<u>shay</u> ehn plen <u>nair</u>

a flower shop.  *une fleuriste.*  oon fler-<u>eest</u>

a flea market.  *un marché aux puces.*
uhn mar-<u>shay</u> oh <u>poos</u>

a dry cleaner.  *un pressing.*  uhn <u>pres</u>-sing

a Laundromat.  *une laverie automatique.*
oon lav-<u>ree</u> oh-toh-mah-<u>teek</u>

a camera store.  *un magasin d'appareils photo.*
uhn mah-gah-<u>zihn</u> dah-pah-<u>ray</u> pho-<u>to</u>

a newsstand.  *un kiosque.*  uhn kee-<u>yahsk</u>

a hair salon.  *un salon de beauté.*
uhn <u>sah</u>-lohn duh <u>boh</u>-tay

a hardware store.  *une quincaillerie.*  oon <u>kan</u>-ky-<u>ree</u>

643.  At the department store.  *Au grand magasin.*
Oh <u>grehn</u> mah-gah-<u>zihn</u>

644.  Where is the . . . department?  *Où se trouve le rayon . . . ?*
Oo <u>suh</u> troov luh ray-<u>ohn</u>

Clothing.  *Vêtements.*  <u>vet</u>-mehn

Shoes.  *Chaussures.*  shoh-<u>ser</u>

Housewares.  *Appareils ménagers.*
ah-pah-<u>ray</u> <u>may</u>-nah-<u>zhay</u>

Electronics.  *Appareils électriques.*
ah-pah-<u>ray</u> <u>ay</u>-lek-<u>treek</u>

Toys.    *Jouets.*    <u>zhoo</u>-ay

Cosmetics.    *Maquillage.*    <u>mah</u>-kee-yahzh

645.    At the clothing store.    *Au magasin de vêtements.*
Oh mah-gah-<u>zihn</u> duh <u>vet</u>-mehn

646.    I'm looking for something . . .
*Je cherche quelque chose de . . .*
Zhuh <u>share-sh</u> kel-kuh <u>shows</u> duh

. . . bigger.    . . . *plus grand.*    ploo <u>grehn</u>

. . . smaller.    . . . *plus petit.*    ploo <u>puh</u>-tee

. . . less expensive.    . . . *moins cher.*    mwehn <u>share</u>

647.    Do you have anything else?    *Vous n'avez rien d'autre?*
Voo nah-vay ree-ehn <u>doht</u>-ruh

648.    May I try this on?    *Je peux l'essayer?*
Zhuh puh <u>less</u>-say-<u>yay</u>

649.    Do you want a different one?    *Vous voulez un(e) autre?*
Voo voo-lay uhn / oon <u>oh</u>-truh

650.    Where is the changing room?
*Où se trouve la cabine d'essayage?*
Oo suh troov lah <u>kah</u>-been <u>dess</u>-say-yahzh

651.    Where can I buy . . . ?    *Où peut-on acheter . . . ?*
Oo puht uhn <u>ahsh</u>-tay

a dress.    *une robe.*    oon <u>ro</u>-buh

a skirt.    *une jupe.*    oon <u>zhoo</u>-puh

some pants.    *des pantalons.*    day <u>pehn</u>-tah-lehn

a shirt.    *une chemise.*    oon <u>shuh</u>-meez

a dress shirt.    *un chemisier.*    uhn <u>shuh</u>-meez-<u>yay</u>

an undershirt.    *un débardeur.*    uhn <u>day</u>-bar-der

a tie.    *une cravate.*    oon krah-<u>vaht</u>

pajamas.    *des pyjamas.*    day <u>pee</u>-zhah-<u>mah</u>

a nightgown.    *une chemise de nuit.*    oon <u>shuh</u>-meez duh <u>nwee</u>

some gloves.    *des gants.*    day <u>gehn</u>

a winter hat.    *un bonnet.*    uhn <u>bohn</u>-nay

a winter coat.   *un manteau.*   uhn <u>mehn</u>-toh

a raincoat.   *un imperméable.*   uhn <u>ihm</u>-pair-may-<u>ab</u>-luh

some boots.   *des bottes.*   day <u>but</u>

some socks.   *des chaussettes.*   day <u>shoh</u>-set

a scarf.   *une écharpe.*   oon <u>ay</u>-sharp

a sweater. (France)   *un pull.*   uhn <u>pool</u>

a sweater. (Québec)   *un chandail.*   uhn <u>shan</u>-dy

652.   At the shoe store.   *Au magasin de chaussures.*
Oh mah-gah-<u>zihn</u> duh shoh-<u>ser</u>

653.   What shoe size do you wear?
*Quelle est votre pointure?*
Kell ay <u>vote</u> pwehn-<u>toor</u>

654.   I wear size . . .   *Ma pointure est le . . . / Je fais du . . .*
Mah pwehn-<u>toor</u> ay / Zhuh fay doo

655.   I'm looking for some . . .   *Je cherche . . .*   Zhuh <u>share-sh</u>

. . . sandals.   . . . *des sandales.*   day sehn-<u>dahl</u>

. . . sneakers.   . . . *des baskets.*   day bas-<u>ket</u>

. . . high heels.   . . . *des escarpins.*   daze <u>es</u>-car-pihn

. . . flip-flops.   . . . *des tongs.*   day tehn-g

656.   At the bookstore.   *À la librairie.*   Ah lah <u>lee</u>-brair-ee

657.   I'm looking for a . . .   *Je cherche . . .*   Zhuh <u>share-sh</u>

. . . a book.   . . . *un livre*   uhn <u>leev</u>-ruh

. . . something in English.   . . . *quelque chose en anglais.*
kell-kuh <u>shows</u> ehn ehn-<u>glay</u>

. . . novel.   . . . *un roman*   uhn <u>row</u>-mehn

. . . a guide book.   . . . *un guide touristique.*
uhn <u>geed</u> too-rees-<u>teek</u>

. . . an English-French dictionary.
. . . *un dictionnaire anglais-français.*
uhn <u>deek</u>-syion-air ehn-<u>glay</u> frehn-say

. . . a children's book.   . . . *un livre pour enfants.*
uhn <u>leev</u>-ruh poor <u>ehn</u>-fehn

. . . a graphic novel.   . . . *une BD.*   oon <u>bay</u>-day

658.    At the stationery store.    *À la papeterie.*
        **Ah lah <u>pah</u>-pet-ree**

659.    I'd like to buy . . .    *J'aimerais acheter . . .*
        **Zhem-<u>ray</u> ahsh-tay**

        . . . a pen.    . . . *un stylo.*    **uhn <u>stee</u>-low**

        . . . a pencil.    . . . *un crayon.*    **uhn <u>kray</u>-ohn**

        . . . a pad of paper.    . . . *un bloc-notes.*    **uhn <u>block</u>-note**

        . . . some envelopes.    . . . *des envelopes.*    **days <u>ehn</u>-vel-ohp**

660.    At the jewelry store.    *À la bijouterie.*
        **Ah lah <u>bee</u>-zhoot-ree**

661.    I'd like to have this watch repaired.
        *Je voudrais faire réparer cette montre.*
        **Zhuh voo-<u>dray</u> fair <u>ray</u>-pah-ray set <u>mohn</u>-truh**

662.    Do you have a battery for this watch?
        *Avez-vous une pile pour cette montre?*
        **Ah-vay voo oon <u>peel</u> poor set <u>mohn</u>-truh?**

663.    I'd like to buy . . .    *J'aimerais acheter . . .*
        **Zhem-<u>ray</u> ahsh-tay**

        . . . a present.    . . . *un cadeau.*    **uhn <u>kah</u>-doh**

        . . . a bracelet.    . . . *un bracelet.*    **uhn <u>brass</u>-lay**

        . . . a ring.    . . . *une bague.*    **oon <u>bahg</u>-uh**

        . . . some earrings.    . . . *des boucles d'oreilles.*
        **day <u>book</u>-luh dore-<u>ay</u>**

        . . . a necklace.    . . . *un collier.*    **uhn <u>kull</u>-yay**

664.    At the tobacco shop.    *Au bureau de tabac.*
        **Oh <u>boo</u>-roh duh <u>tah</u>-bah**

665.    A pack of cigarettes, please.    *Un paquet de cigarettes.*
        **Uhn <u>pah</u>-kay duh <u>seeg</u>-ah-ret**

666.    A lighter.    *Un briquet.*    **Uhn <u>bree</u>-kay**

667.    Some matches.    *Des allumettes.*    **Days <u>ahl</u>-oo-met**

668.  Some stamps.  *Des timbres.*  **Day <u>tihm</u>-bruh**

669.  At the bakery.  *À la boulangerie.*  **Ah lah <u>boo</u>-lehn-zhree**

670.  I'd like . . .  *Je voudrais . . .*  **Zhuh-voo-<u>dray</u>**

. . . a loaf of French bread.  . . . *une baguette.*
**oon <u>bah</u>-get**

. . . half a loaf of French bread.  . . . *une demi-baguette.*
**oon <u>duh</u>-mee-<u>bah</u>-get**

. . . some rolls.  . . . *des petits pains.*  **day <u>puh</u>-tee pihn**

. . . a loaf of whole-wheat bread.  . . . *un pain complet.*
**uhn <u>pihn</u> kuhm-<u>play</u>**

671.  At the pastry shop.  *À la patisserie.*  **Ah lah <u>pah</u>-tee-sree**

672.  We'd like . . .  *On voudrait . . .*  **Ohn <u>voo</u>-dray**

. . . two croissants.  . . . *deux croissants.*  **duh <u>kwah</u>-sehn**

. . . a chocolate croissant.  . . . *un croissant au chocolat.*
**uhn <u>kwah</u>-sehn oh <u>shoh</u>-koh-<u>lah</u>**

. . . a raisin bun.  . . . *un pain au raisin.*
**uhn <u>pihn</u> oh <u>ray</u>-zihn**

. . . some pastries.  . . . *des patisseries.*  **day <u>pah</u>-tee-sree**

. . . some cookies.  . . . *des biscuits.*  **day <u>bees</u>-kwee**

673.  At the supermarket.  *Au supermarché.*
**Oh <u>soo</u>-pair-mar-<u>shay</u>**

674.  Where is the . . . section?  *Où se trouve le rayon . . . ?*
**Oo suh troov luh <u>ray</u>-ohn**

Cheese.  *Fromage.*  **fro-<u>mah-zh</u>**

Wine.  *Vin et spiritueux.*  **vihn ay <u>spee</u>-ree-too-uh**

Candy.  *Confiserie.*  **kuhn-<u>fee</u>-sree**

Meat.  *Viande.*  **vee-<u>ehn</u>-duh**

Fish.  *Poisson.*  **<u>pwah</u>-sohn**

Dairy.  *Produits laitiers.*  **<u>pro</u>-dwee <u>lay</u>-tee-ay**

675.  At the deli.  *Chez le traiteur.*  **Shay luh tret-<u>ter</u>**

676.   Do you have take-out?     *Vous avez des plats à emporter?*
       **Voo zah-vay day <u>plah</u> ah <u>ehm</u>-pore-tay**

677.   At the flower shop.     *Chez le fleuriste.*     **Shay luh fler-<u>eest</u>**

678.   Do you like flowers?
       *Vous aimez les fleurs?     Tu aimes les fleurs?*
       **Vooz <u>ay</u>-may / Too <u>ehm</u> lay fler**

679.   I'd like to buy a bouquet of flowers.
       *J'aimerais acheter un bouquet de fleurs.*
       **Zhem-<u>ray</u> <u>ahsh</u>-tay uhn <u>boo</u>-kay duh <u>fler</u>**

680.   You can choose them.     *Vous pouvez les choisir.*
       **Voo poo-vay lay <u>shwah</u>-zeer**

681.   I'd like a combination of flowers.
       *J'aimerais un bouquet de fleurs assorties.*
       **Zhem-<u>ray</u> uhn <u>boo</u>-kay day <u>fler</u> ah-sore-<u>tee</u>**

682.   I would like . . .     *Je voudrais . . .*     **Zhuh voo-<u>dray</u>**

       . . . some roses.     . . . *des roses.*     **day <u>roze</u>**

       . . . some tulips.     . . . *des tulipes.*     **day too-<u>leep</u>**

       . . . some daisies.     . . . *des marguerites.*     **day mar-<u>guhr</u>-reet**

       . . . some peonies.     . . . *des pivoines.*     **day <u>peev</u>-vwehn**

683.   Will I need to change the water daily?
       *Faut-il changer l'eau chaque jour?*
       **Foh-teel <u>shehn</u>-zhay loh <u>shahk</u> zhoor**

684.   Can you wrap these in paper?     *Pouvez-vous les emballer?*
       **Poo-vay voo <u>laze</u> ehm-bahl-<u>lay</u>**

685.   I'd like to send some flowers . . .
       *J'aimerais envoyer des fleurs . . .*
       **Zhem-<u>ray</u> <u>ehn</u>-vwah-yay day <u>fler</u>**

       . . . to this address.     . . . *à cette adresse.*     **ah set ah-<u>dress</u>**

       . . . to this person.     . . . *à cette personne.*     **ah set pair-<u>sun</u>**

686.   I'd like a house plant.     *J'aimerais une plante.*
       **Zhem-<u>ray</u> oon <u>plehn</u>-tuh**

687.  Do you sell planted flowers?
*Vendez-vous des fleurs en pots?*
**Vehn-day voo day <u>fler</u> ehn poh**

688.  At the dry cleaners.    *Au pressing.*    **Oh <u>pres</u>-sing**

689.  Do you have a laundry service?
*Avez-vous un service de blanchisserie?*
**Ah-vay vooz uhn <u>sair</u>-vees duh <u>blan</u>-shees-<u>ree</u>**

690.  When will my things be ready?
*Quand est-ce que mes affaires seront prêtes?*
**Kehn ess kuh <u>maze</u> ah-<u>fair</u> suhr-ohn <u>prett</u>**

691.  Can you iron these?
*Pouvez-vous faire repasser ces vêtements?*
**Poo-vay voo fair <u>ruh</u>-pass-say say <u>vet</u>-mehn**

692.  Can you shorten these pants?
*Pouvez-vous raccourcir ce pantalon?*
**Poo-vay voo <u>rah</u>-koor-seer suh <u>pehn</u>-tah-lohn**

693.  Do you do mending?
*Est-ce que vous faîtes des petites réparations?*
**Ess kuh voo <u>fet</u> day <u>puh</u>-teet <u>ray</u>-pahr-ah-syion**

694.  At the Laundromat. (France)    *À la laverie automatique.*
**Ah lah <u>lahv</u>-ree <u>oh</u>-toh-mah-<u>teek</u>**

695.  At the Laundromat. (Québec)    *À la launderette.*
**Ah lah <u>lohn</u>-dret**

696.  What coins do I need for these machines?
*Quelles pièces faut-il pour ces machines?*
**Kell pee-<u>yes</u> foh-teel poor say <u>mah</u>-sheen**

697.  Where can I buy some detergent?
*Où peut-on acheter de la lessive?*
**Oo puh-tohn <u>ahsh</u>-tay duh lah less-<u>eev</u>**

698.  Is there any powder detergent?
*Est-ce qu'il y a de la lessive en poudre?*
**Ess keel <u>yah</u> duh lah less-<u>eev</u> ehn <u>poo</u>-druh**

699. Where can I dry my clothes?
*Où est-ce que je peux faire sécher mon linge?*
Oo ess kuh zhuh puh fair <u>say</u>-shay mohn <u>lihnzh</u>

700. At the camera store.    *Au magasin d'appareils photo.*
Oh mah-gah-<u>zihn</u> dah-pah-<u>ray</u> pho-<u>to</u>

701. I'm looking for . . .    *Je cherche . . .*    Zhuh <u>share-sh</u>
. . . . a digital camera.    *. . . un appareil numérique.*
uhn ah-pah-<u>ray</u> noo-may-<u>reek</u>

. . . film for this camera.
*. . . une pellicule pour cet appareil photo.*
oon pay-leel-<u>kool</u> poor set ah-pah-<u>ray</u> pho-<u>to</u>

. . . batteries for my camera.
*. . . des piles pour mon appareil photo.*
day <u>peel</u> poor mohn ah-pah-<u>ray</u> pho-<u>to</u>

702. Can you suggest a good . . . ?
*Pouvez-vous suggérer un bon . . . ?*
Poo-vay voo <u>soog</u>-zhay-ray uhn <u>bohn</u>

. . . point-and-shoot camera.    *. . . appareil compact.*
ah-pah-<u>ray</u> kuhm-<u>pakt</u>

. . . a mid-range camera.    *. . . appareil bridge.*
ah-pah-<u>ray</u> bree-dzh

. . . a DSLR camera.    *. . . appareil reflex.*
ah-pah-<u>ray</u> <u>ruh</u>-flex

703. Can this be used abroad?    *Ceci peut s'utiliser à l'étranger?*
Suh-see puh <u>soot</u>-ee-lee-zay ah <u>lay</u>-tran-<u>zhay</u>

704. Will I need a different plug / adaptor?
*Est-ce que j'aurai besoin d'une prise différente?*
Ess kuh zhore-ay <u>buh</u>-zwehn doon preez <u>dif</u>-fay-<u>rehnt</u>

705. What lenses do you carry?
*Qu'est-ce que vous avez comme objectifs?*
Kess kuh vooz ah-vay kum <u>ob</u>-zhek-<u>teef</u>

706. Do you sell cleaning kits?
*Vendez-vous des kits de nettoyage?*
Vehn-day voo day <u>keet</u> duh neh-twah-<u>yahzh</u>

707. At the newsstand. *Au kiosque.* **Oh kee-<u>yahsk</u>**

708. A newspaper, please. *Un journal, s'il vous plaît.*
**Uhn zhoor-<u>nal</u> see voo <u>play</u>**

709. Where are the English language magazines?
*Où sont les publications anglophones?*
**Oo sohn lay <u>poob</u>-lee-ka-syion ehn-glow-<u>phone</u>**

710. At the hair salon. *Chez le coiffeur.* **Shay luh <u>kwah</u>-foor**

711. I'd like to make an appointment.
*Je voudrais prendre un rendez-vous.*
**Zhuh voo-dray <u>prehn</u>-druh uhn <u>rehn</u>-day-<u>voo</u>**

712. Do you take walk-ins? *Vous prenez sans rendez-vous?*
**Voo pruh-nay <u>sehn</u> rehn-day-<u>voo</u>**

713. I'd like . . . *Je voudrais . . .* **Zhuh voo-<u>dray</u>**

. . . a haircut. . . . *une coupe de cheveux.*
**oon <u>koop</u> duh shuh-<u>vuh</u>**

. . . a blow-out. . . . *un brushing.* **uhn <u>brush</u>-ing**

. . . highlights. . . . *des mèches.* **day <u>mesh</u>**

. . . just a shampoo. . . . *juste un shampooing.*
**zhoost uhn shamp-<u>pwehn</u>**

# MEASUREMENTS

714. 500 grams of . . . *500 grammes de . . .*
**Sank-sehn <u>grahm</u> duh**

715. A kilo of . . . *Un kilo de . . .* **Uhn <u>kee</u>-loh duh**

716. A half-kilo of . . . *Un demi-kilo de . . .*
**Uhn <u>duh</u>-mee <u>kee</u>-loh duh**

717. A bottle of . . . *Une bouteille de . . .* **Oon boo-<u>tay</u> duh**

718. A half-bottle of . . . *Une demi-bouteille de . . .*
**Oon <u>duh</u>-mee boo-<u>tay</u> duh**

719. A liter of . . . *Un litre de . . .* **Uhn <u>leet</u>-ruh duh**

720. A glass of . . . *Un verre de . . .* **Uhn <u>vair</u> duh**

721. A slice of . . . (pizza)  *Une tranche de . . .*
     Oon <u>transh</u> duh

722. A package of . . .  *Une boîte de . . .*  Oon <u>bwaht</u> duh

723. A piece of . . . (meat)  *Un morceau de . . .*
     Uhn <u>more</u>-soh duh

724. A little bit of . . .  *Un petit peu de . . .*
     Uhn <u>puh</u>-tee <u>puh</u> duh

725. A box of . . .  *Une boîte de . . .*  Oon <u>bwaht</u> duh

726. A handful of . . .  *Une poignée de . . .*
     Oon <u>pwa</u>-nyay duh

727. A can of . . .  *Une boîte de . . .*  Oon <u>bwaht</u> duh

728. A dozen . . .  *Une douzaine de . . .*  Oon doo-<u>zen</u> duh

729. A jar of . . .  *Un pot de . . .*  Uhn <u>poh</u> duh

730. More . . .  *Encore . . .*  Ehn-<u>kore</u>

731. Less . . .  *Moins . . .*  Mwehn

732. That's enough.  *C'est assez.*  Set ah-<u>say</u>

# COLORS

733. Blue.  *Bleu(e).*  Bluh

734. Green.  *Vert(e).*  Vair/vairte

735. Red.  *Rouge.*  Roozh

736. White.  *Blanc(he).*  Blehn/blehnsh

737. Purple.  *Violet(te).*  Vee-oh-<u>lay</u>/vee-oh-<u>let</u>

738. Black.  *Noir(e).*  Nwahr

739. Brown.  *Marron.*  <u>Mah</u>-ron

740. Yellow.  *Jaune.*  <u>Zhoh</u>-nuh

741. Orange.  *Orange.*  **Or-<u>ehnzh</u>**

742. Pink.  *Rose.*  **Roze**

743. Maybe another color?  *Une autre couleur, peut-être?*
**Oon <u>oht</u> koo-<u>ler</u> puh-<u>tet</u>-ruh**

744. I love this color.  *J'adore cette couleur.*
**Zhah-<u>dore</u> set coo-<u>ler</u>**

745. Something darker?  *Quelque chose de plus foncé?*
**Kel-kuh <u>shows</u> duh ploo <u>fohn</u>-say**

746. Something lighter?  *Quelque chose de plus clair?*
**Kel-kuh <u>shows</u> duh ploo <u>klare</u>**

747. Something striped?  *Quelque chose de rayé?*
**Kel-kuh <u>shows</u> duh <u>ray</u>-yay**

748. Something with polka dots?  *Quelque chose à pois?*
**Kel-kuh <u>shows</u> ah <u>pwah</u>**

# Chapter 6
## Health and Well-being

If you are feeling under the weather while traveling, make your first stop *la pharmacie* (the pharmacy). The role of the pharmacy is quite different from the American counterpart, as people tend to first consult pharmacists for health issues before contacting their doctor. At the pharmacy, you'll be able to get advice and fill prescriptions, as well as buy over-the-counter medications. Note that unlike the United States, these medications aren't available in supermarkets. If you need after-hours attention, look for a *pharmacie de garde* or *pharmacie de nuit*. In France, pharmacies are easily recognizable by the neon-green cross that identifies them.

## AT THE PHARMACY

749. Where is the nearest pharmacy?
*Où se trouve la pharmacie la plus proche?*
**Oo suh troov lah far-mah-<u>see</u> lah ploo <u>proh-sh</u>**

750. Is there a 24-hour pharmacy nearby?
*Est-ce qu'il y a une pharmace de garde près d'ici?*
**Ess keel <u>yah</u> oon far-mah-<u>see</u> duh <u>gard</u> pray dee-<u>see</u>**

751. Do I need a prescription?
*Est-ce que j'ai besoin d'une ordonnance?*
**Ess kuh zhay <u>buh</u>-zwehn doon <u>ore</u>-dun-<u>nehns</u>**

752. I don't have a prescription.    *Je n'ai pas d'ordonnance.*
**Zhuh nay <u>pah</u> <u>dore</u>-dun-<u>nehns</u>**

753. My prescription is from an American doctor.
*Mon ordonnance est faite par un médecin américain.*
**Mohn ore-dun-nehns ay fet par uhn made-sihn ah-mary-kihn**

754. Do you have a sample of this?
*Avez-vous un échantillon de cela?*
**Ah-vay voo uhn ay-shehn-ti-yehn duh suh-lah**

755. Is this product appropriate for children?
*Est-ce que ce produit s'utilise pour les enfants?*
**Ess kuh suh pro-dwee soo-tee-leez poor laze ehn-fehn**

756. What are the potential side-effects of this?
*Quels sont les effets secondaires potentiels de ceci?*
**Kel sohn lay zay-fay suh-kuhn-dare poh-tahn-see-ell duh suh-see**

757. I'd like to buy . . .     *J'aimerais acheter . . .*
**Zhem-ray ahsh-tay**

   . . . some aspirin.     . . . *de l'aspirine.*     duh **lass-pee-reen**

   . . . some vitamins.     . . . *des vitamines.*     day **vee-tah-meen**

   . . . some band aids.     . . . *des pansements.*     day **pans-mehn**

   . . . some tissues.     . . . *des mouchoirs.*     day moo-**shwahr**

758. Can you recommend a good . . . ?
*Pouvez-vous recommander un bon . . . ?*
**Poo-vay voo ruh-koh-mehn-day uhn bohn**

   . . . shampoo.     . . . *shampooing.*     shahm-**pwehn**

   . . . soap.     . . . *savon.*     sah-**vohn**

759. What do you have in the way of . . . ?
*Qu'est-ce que vous avez comme . . . ?*
**Kess kuh voo zah-vay kum**

   . . . makeup.     . . . *maquillage.*     mah-kee-**yahzh**

   . . . perfume.     . . . *parfum.*     par-**fihm**

760. I need . . .     *J'ai besoin . . .*     Zhay **buh-zwehn**

   . . . a toothbrush.     . . . *d'une brosse à dents.*
**doon bruss ah dehn**

   . . . some toothpaste.     . . . *du dentifrice.*
**doo dehn-tee-frees**

... some dental floss.    ... *du fil dentaire.*
**doo feel <u>dehn</u>-tare**

... some shaving cream.    ... *de la crème à raser.*
**duh lah <u>krem</u> ah <u>rah</u>-zay**

761.   Do you carry this brand of ... ?
*Est-ce que vous vendez cette marque de ... ?*
**Ess kuh voo <u>vehn</u>-day set <u>mark</u> duh**

... cleanser.    ... *nettoyant.*    **neh-twah-<u>yehn</u>**

... razor.    ... *rasoir.*    **<u>ra</u>-zwahr**

762.   I'm looking for some medication for ...
*Je cherche un médicament contre ...*
**Zhuh <u>share-sh</u> uhn may-dee-kah-<u>mehn</u> <u>kohn</u>-truh**

... a headache.    ... *le mal de tête.*    **luh <u>mahl</u> duh <u>tet</u>**

... pain.    ... *la douleur.*    **lah doo-<u>ler</u>**

... a cold.    ... *le rhume.*    **luh <u>room</u>**

... the flu.    ... *la grippe.*    **lah <u>greep</u>**

... allergies.    ... *les allergies.*    **laze <u>ah</u>-lair-<u>zhee</u>**

... a cough.    ... *la toux.*    **lah <u>too</u>**

... a bee sting.    ... *une piqûre d'abeille.*
**oon pee-<u>koor</u> dah-<u>bay</u>**

... cramps.    ... *les douleurs.*    **lay doo-<u>ler</u>**

763.   I need ...    *J'ai besoin ...*    **Zhay <u>buh</u>-zwehn**

... some pills.    ... *de comprimés.*    **duh <u>kohm</u>-pree-<u>may</u>**

... a suppository.    ... *d'un suppositoire.*
**duhn <u>soo</u>-poh-zee-<u>twahr</u>**

... a cream.    ... *d'une crème.*    **doon <u>krem</u>**

... tampons.    ... *de tampons.*    **duh <u>tahm</u>-pohn**

... feminine napkins.    ... *de serviettes hygiéniques.*
**duh <u>sair</u>-vee-et <u>ee</u>-zhen-<u>eek</u>**

... condoms.    ... *de préservatifs.*    **duh <u>pray</u>-zair-vah-<u>teef</u>**

764.   I need to replace my contact lenses.
*J'ai besoin de faire remplacer mes lentilles.*
**Zhay <u>buh</u>-zwehn duh fair <u>rahm</u>-plah-say may <u>lehn</u>-tee**

765. What contact-lens solution do you have?
*Qu'est-ce que vous avez comme solution d'entretien pour lentilles?*
**Kess kuh voo <u>zah</u>-vay kuhm <u>soh</u>-loo-syion <u>dehn</u>-truh-ti-<u>yen</u>
poor <u>lehn</u>-tee**

766. What kind of diapers do you sell?
*Qu'est-ce que vous avez comme couches?*
**Kess kuh voo <u>zah</u>-vay kuhm <u>koosh</u>?**

767. Do you sell baby wipes, too?
*Est-ce que vous vendez des lingettes aussi?*
**Ess kuh voo <u>vehn</u>-day day lihnzh-<u>et</u> oh-<u>see</u>**

768. Do you have baby bottles like this one?
*Est-ce que vous avez des biberons comme celui-ci?*
**Ess kuh voo <u>zah</u>-vay day <u>beeb</u>-rone kuhm suh-lwee-<u>see</u>**

769. Please show me what you have in the way of sunscreen.
*Montrez-moi ce que vous avez comme écran solaire.*
**Mehn-tray <u>mwah</u> suh kuh voo <u>zah</u>-vay kuhm <u>ay</u>-krehn
soh-<u>lair</u>**

770. I'd like to buy a . . .    *J'aimerais acheter . . .*
**Zhem-<u>ray</u> ahsh-<u>tay</u>**

   . . . a self-tanner.    . . . *un autobronzant.*
   **uhn <u>oh</u>-toh <u>brehnz</u>-ehn**

   . . . an after-sun cream.    . . . *une crème après-soleil.*
   **oon <u>krem</u> ah-<u>pray</u> soh-<u>lay</u>**

771. Do you have something with a stronger SPF?
*Avez-vous quelque chose avec une protection plus forte?*
**Ah-vay voo <u>kel</u>-kuh <u>shows</u> ah-<u>vek</u> oon <u>proh</u>-tek-syion ploo <u>fort</u>**

772. Do you have something for a sunburn?
*Est-ce que vous avez quelque chose pour un coup de soleil?*
**Ess kuh voo <u>zah</u>-vay <u>kel</u>-kuh <u>shows</u> poor uhn <u>koo</u> duh <u>soh</u>-lay**

## SEEING A DOCTOR

773. I am (very) sick.    *Je suis (très) malade.*
**<u>Zhuh</u> swee (<u>tray</u>) mah-<u>lahd</u>**

774. I need to see the doctor.    *J'ai besoin d'une consultation.*
**Zhay <u>buh</u>-zwehn doon <u>kone</u>-sul-tah-<u>syion</u>**

775. Where does it hurt?    *Où avez-vous mal?*
**Oo <u>ah</u>-vay-voo <u>mahl</u>?**

776. I have . . .    *J'ai . . .*    **Zhay**
. . . a headache.    . . . *mal à la tête.*    **mahl ah lah <u>tet</u>**
. . . a sore throat.    . . . *mal à la gorge.*    **mahl ah lah <u>gorzh</u>**
. . . an earache.    . . . *une otite.*    **oon <u>oh</u>-teet**
. . . a migraine.    . . . *une migraine.*    **oon mee-<u>gren</u>**
. . . a cold.    . . . *un rhume.*    **uhn <u>roohm</u>**

777. Look, it's . . .    *Regardez, c'est . . .*    **<u>Ruh</u>-gar-day <u>say</u>**
. . . infected.    . . . *infecté.*    **<u>ehn</u>-fek-tay**
. . . swollen.    . . . *enflé.*    **<u>ehn</u>-flay**

778. I think I have the flu.    *Je crois avoir la grippe.*
**Zhuh kwah <u>ahv</u>-wahr lah <u>greep</u>**

779. I have indigestion.    *J'ai une indigestion.*
**Zhay oon <u>ihn</u>-dee-zhess-<u>tyion</u>**

780. I have a rash.    *J'ai une eruption cutanée.*
**Zhay oon <u>ay</u>-roop-syion <u>koo</u>-tehn-<u>ay</u>**

781. I think I . . .    *Je me suis peut-être . . .*
**<u>Zhuh</u> muh swee puh-<u>tet</u>-ruh**
. . . broke my arm.    . . . *cassé le bras.*    **<u>kah</u>-say luh <u>brah</u>**
. . . broke my leg.    . . . *cassé la jambe.*
**<u>kah</u>-say lah <u>zhahm</u>-buh**
. . . twisted my ankle.    . . . *tordu la cheville.*
**<u>tore</u>-doo lah <u>shuh</u>-vee**
. . . hurt myself.    . . . *blessé.*    **<u>bless</u>-say**

782. My child is sick.    *Mon enfant est malade.*
**Mohn <u>ehn</u>-fehn ay mah-<u>lahd</u>**

783. I need a doctor.    *J'ai besoin d'un médecin.*
**Zhay <u>buh</u>-zwehn duhn <u>made</u>-sihn**

784. May I please speak to a nurse?
*Est-ce que je peux parler à une infirmière?*
**Ess kuh zhuh puh par-lay ah oon ihn-fair-mee-air?**

785. Where is the aide? *Où est l'aide-soignante?*
**Oo ay led swehn-yehnt**

786. Please take me to . . . *Veuillez m'emmener . . .*
**Vuh-yay mehm-nay**

. . . a hospital. . . . *à l'hôpital.* **ah loh-pee-tahl**

. . . the emergency room. . . . *à la salle des urgences.*
**ah lah sahl daze oorzh-ehns**

. . . a pharmacy. . . . *à la pharmacie.* **ah lah far-mah-see**

. . . a 24-hour pharmacy. . . . *à la pharmacie de garde.*
**ah lah far-mah-see duh gard**

787. Does he need to go to the hospital?
*Faut-il le transporter à l'hôpital?*
**Foh-teel luh trehns-pore-tay ah loh-pee-tahl**

788. I'm having intestinal problems.
*J'ai des problèmes intestinaux.*
**Zhay day proh-blemz ihn-tess-tee-noh**

789. I have high blood pressure.
*J'ai une hypertension artérielle.*
**Zhay oon ee-pair-tehn-syion ar-tare-ee-el**

790. Will you need to draw blood?
*Est-ce que vous aurez besoin de faire une prise de sang?*
**Ess kuh vooz ore-ray buh-zwehn duh fair oon preez duh sehn**

791. I am taking this medication. *Je prends ce médicament.*
**Zhuh prehn suh may-dee-kah-mehn**

792. I am diabetic. *Je suis diabétique.*
**Zhuh swee dee-yah-bet-eek**

793. I am pregnant. *Je suis enceinte.*
**Zhuh sweez ehn-sihnt**

794. I am allergic to aspirin. *Je suis allergique à l'aspirine.*
**Zhuh sweez ah-lair-zheek ah lahs-pee-reen**

795. I'm on the pill.    *Je prends la pilule.*
     **Zhuh <u>prehn</u> lah <u>pee</u>-lool**

796. I need antibiotics.    *J'ai besoin d'antibiotiques.*
     **Zhay <u>buh</u>-zwehn <u>dan-tee</u>-bee-oh-<u>teek</u>**

797. Is it serious?    *C'est grave?*    **Say <u>grav</u>**

798. How are you feeling?    *Comment vous sentez–vous?*
     **Kuh-muh voo <u>sehn</u>-tay <u>voo</u>**

799. I'm feeling better, thanks.    *Je vais mieux, merci.*
     **Zhuh vay <u>myuh</u> mare-<u>see</u>**

800. I don't feel well.    *Je me sens mal.*
     **Zhuh <u>muh</u> sehn <u>mahl</u>**

801. I'm feeling dizzy.    *J'ai la tête qui tourne.*
     **Zhay lah <u>tet</u> kee <u>toor</u>-nuh**

802. I feel like throwing up.    *Je suis sur le point de vomir.*
     **Zhuh <u>swee</u> soor luh <u>pwehn</u> duh <u>voh</u>-meer**

803. The situation is getting worse.    *La situation s'empire.*
     **Lah <u>see</u>-too-ah-<u>syion</u> sehm-<u>peer</u>**

804. I'm resting.    *Je me repose.*    **<u>Zhuh</u> muh ruh-<u>poze</u>**

805. May I have a receipt for my health insurance?
     *Il me faut un reçu pour l'assurance.*
     **Eel muh <u>foh</u> uhn <u>ruh</u>-soo poor <u>lass</u>-oo-<u>rehns</u>**

## SEEING A DENTIST

806. Can you recommend a good dentist?
     *Pouvez-vous recommander un bon dentiste?*
     **Poo-vay voo <u>ruh</u>-koh-mehn-<u>day</u> uhn <u>bohn</u> dehn-<u>teest</u>**

807. I have a toothache.    *J'ai mal aux dents.*
     **Zhay <u>mahl</u> oh <u>dehn</u>**

808. Do I have a cavity?    *Est-ce que j'ai une carie?*
     **Ess kuh <u>zhay</u> oon <u>kah</u>-ree**

809.   I think I have an abcess.    *Je crois avoir un abcès.*
       Zhuh <u>kwah</u> ahv-<u>wahr</u> uhn <u>ahb</u>-say

810.   I think I lost a crown.    *Je crois avoir perdu une couronne.*
       Zhuh <u>kwah</u> ahv-<u>wahr</u> pair-dew oon koo-<u>run</u>

811.   It hurts!    *Ça fait mal!*    Sah fay <u>mahl</u>

812.   Can you . . . ?    *Pouvez-vous . . . ?*    Poo-vay <u>voo</u>
       . . . give me a filling.    . . . *me faire un plombage.*
       muh fair uhn <u>plohm</u>-bahzh
       . . . give me a temporary filling.
       . . . *me faire un plombage momentané.*
       muh fair uhn <u>plohm</u>-bahzh <u>moh</u>-mehn-tah-<u>nay</u>
       . . . give me something for the pain.
       . . . *me donner quelque chose contre la douleur.*
       muh duh-<u>nay</u> kel-kuh <u>shows</u> kone-truh lah dool-<u>er</u>

813.   Does it need to be pulled?    *Faut-il l'arracher?*
       Foh-teel <u>lah</u>-rah-<u>shay</u>

814.   I need to have my dentures fixed.
       *J'ai besoin de faire réparer mon dentier.*
       Zhay <u>buh</u>-zwehn duh <u>fair</u> <u>ray</u>-pah-<u>ray</u> moh <u>dent</u>-yay

815.   He/she wears braces.    *Il/elle porte un appareil dentaire.*
       Eel / ell <u>port</u> uhn <u>ah</u>-pah-<u>ray</u> dehn-<u>tair</u>

# Chapter 7
## Communications

## THE POST OFFICE

816.  Where is the nearest post office?
      *Où est le bureau de poste le plus proche?*
      **Oo ay luh <u>boo</u>-roh duh <u>pust</u> luh ploo <u>proh-sh</u>**

817.  Is there a mailbox nearby?
      *Il y a une boîte aux lettres près d'ici?*
      **Eel yah oon <u>bwaht</u> oh <u>lett</u>-ruh pray dee-<u>see</u>**

818.  I need to mail ...      *J'ai besoin d'envoyer ...*
      **Zhay <u>buh</u>-zwehn <u>dehn</u>-vwah-yay**

      ... a letter.      ... *une lettre.*      **oon <u>lett</u>-ruh**

      ... a postcard.      ..,. *une carte postale.*      **oon <u>kart</u> poh-<u>stahl</u>**

      ... a money order.      ... *un mandat.*      **uhn <u>mehn</u>-dah**

      ... a package.      ... *un colis.*      **uhn <u>koh</u>-lee**

819.  I'd like to buy some stamps.      *J'aimerais acheter des timbres.*
      **Zhem-<u>ray</u> <u>ahsh</u>-tay day <u>tihm</u>-bruh**

820.  I need to send a registered letter.
      *J'ai besoin d'envoyer une lettre recommandée.*
      **Zhay <u>buh</u>-zhwehn <u>dehnv</u>-wyah-yay oon <u>lett</u>-ruh <u>ruh</u>-koh-mehn-<u>day</u>**

821.  What's the postage for the U.S.?      *C'est combien pour les
      États-Unis?*      **Say kuhm-<u>byehn</u> poor <u>laze</u> ay-tahz oo-<u>nee</u>**

## THE TELEPHONE

822. Where can I make a phone call?
*Où est-ce que je peux donner un coup de fil?*
**Oo ess kuh zhuh <u>puh</u> duhn-<u>nay</u> uhn <u>koo</u> duh <u>feel</u>**

823. How much does it cost to call the U.S.?
*C'est combien pour appeler les États-Unis?*
**Say kuhm-<u>byehn</u> poor <u>ahp</u>-lay <u>laze</u> ay-tahz oo-<u>nee</u>**

824. I'd like to buy a phone card, please.
*Une télécarte, s'il vous plaît.*  **Oon <u>tay</u>-lay-<u>kart</u>, see voo <u>play</u>**

825. Do you have a phonebook?  *Avez-vous un annuaire?*
**Ah-vay <u>voo</u> uhn ah-noo-<u>air</u>**

826. I'd like to phone home.  *Je voudrais appeler chez moi.*
**Zhuh voo-<u>dray</u> <u>ahp</u>-lay <u>shay</u> mwah**

827. I'd like to make a collect call.  *J'aimerais appeler en pcv.*
**Zhem-<u>ray</u> <u>ahp</u>-lay ehn <u>pay</u>-say-vay**

828. What is the number here?
*Quel est le numéro de téléphone ici?*
**<u>Kel</u> ay luh <u>noo</u>-may-<u>roh</u> duh <u>tay</u>-lay-fun ee-<u>see</u>**

829. Do you have the number for the American consulate?
*Avez-vous le numéro de telephone pour le consulat américain?*
**Ah-vay <u>voo</u> luh noo-may-<u>roh</u> duh tay-lay-fun por luh <u>kohn</u>-suh-lah ah-mary-<u>kihn</u>**

830. I'd like to buy a cell phone.
*J'aimerais acheter un téléphone portable.*
**Zhem-<u>ray</u> <u>ahsh</u>-tay uhn <u>tay</u>-lay-fun por-<u>tahb</u>-luh**

831. Is there a contract?  *Y a-t-il un contrat?*
**Ee yah-teel uhn kohn-<u>trah</u>**

832. My number is . . .  *Mon numéro est le . . .*
**Mohn noo-may-<u>roh</u> ay luh**

833. I'd like to speak to . . .  *Je voudrais parler à . . .*
**Zhuh voo-<u>dray</u> pah-<u>lay</u> ah**

834.  Hello?    *Âllo?*    **Ah-loh**

835.  Who is calling?    *C'est de la part de qui?*
      **Say duh lah par duh kee**

836.  It's Bruce calling.    *C'est Bruce à l'appareil.*
      **Say Bruce ah lah-par-ay.**

837.  I'll put you through to him/her.    *Je vous le/la passe.*
      **Zhuh voo luh/lah pass**

838.  One moment, please.    *Un instant, s'il vous plaît.*
      **Uhn ihn-stehn see voo play**

839.  Please hold on.    *Patientez, s'il vous plaît.*
      **Pass-yen-tay see voo play**

840.  Can you call back?    *Vous pouvez rappeller?*
      **Voo poo-vay rahp-lay**

841.  It's busy.    *C'est occupé.*    **Say oh-koo-pay**

842.  Would you like to leave a message?
      *Voulez-vous laisser un message?*
      **Voo-lay voo les-say uhn mess-ahzh**

843.  I'll call back later.    *Je vais rappeler plus tard.*
      **Zhuh vay rahp-lay ploo tar**

844.  We were cut off.    *Nous avons été coupés.*
      **Nooz ahv-uhn ay-tay koo-pay**

845.  I can't get the call to go through.
      *Je ne peux pas avoir le numéro.*
      **Zhuh nuh puh pah ahv-wahr luh noo-may-roh**

## THE INTERNET AND COMPUTERS

846.  A computer.    *Un ordinateur.*    **Uhn or-dee-nah-tuhr**

847.  A printer.    *Une imprimante.*    **Oon ihm-pree-mehnte**

848.  An ink cartridge.    *Une cartouche d'encre.*
      **Oon kar-toosh dehn-kruh**

849. A laptop.  *Un ordinateur portable.*
     **Uhn <u>or</u>-dee-nah-<u>tuhr</u> por-<u>tah</u>-bluh**

850. A battery.  *Une pile.*  **Oon <u>peel</u>**

851. A battery charger.  *Un chargeur pour piles.*
     **Uhn shar-<u>zher</u> poor <u>peel</u>**

852. A power cord.  *Un cordon.*  **Uhn kore-<u>dohn</u>**

853. A cable.  *Un câble.*  **Uhn <u>ka</u>-bluh**

854. Where can I get a Wi-Fi connection?
     *Où je peux me connecter en Wi-Fi?*
     **Oo zhuh <u>puh</u> muh <u>kuhn</u>-ek-<u>tay</u> ehn <u>wee</u>-fee**

855. Is there an Internet café nearby?
     *Il y a un cyber café près d'ici?*
     **Eel <u>yah</u> uhn <u>see</u>-bair <u>kah</u>-fay pray dee-<u>see</u>**

856. Can I go online?  *Je peux aller en ligne?*
     **Zhuh puh <u>ah</u>-lay ehn <u>lee</u>-nyuh**

857. Do you have a high-speed Internet connection?
     *Vous avez une connexion Internet haut-débit?*
     **Voo <u>zah</u>-vay <u>oon</u> koh-nex-<u>syion</u> ihn-tair-<u>net</u> oh-day-<u>bee</u>**

858. Is there a computer I can use?
     *Est-ce qu'il y a un ordinateur que je peux utiliser?*
     **Ess keel <u>yah</u> uhn <u>ore</u>-dee-nah-<u>tuhr</u> kuh zhuh <u>puh</u>
     oo-tee-lee-<u>zay</u>**

859. Do you have a laptop?  *Vous avez un ordinateur portable?*
     **Vooz <u>ah</u>-vay uhn <u>ore</u>-dee-nah-<u>tuhr</u> pore-<u>tah</u>-bluh**

860. Does this computer have an Internet connection?
     *Est-ce que cet ordinateur a une connexion Internet?*
     **Ess <u>kuh</u> set <u>ore</u>-dee-nah-<u>tuhr</u> ah <u>oon</u> koh-nex-<u>syion</u>
     ihn-tair-<u>net</u>**

861. I'd like to send an email.  *Je voudrais envoyer un mail.*
     **Zhuh voo-<u>dray</u> <u>ehn</u>-vwah-<u>yay</u> uhn <u>mel</u>**

862. Do you have a website?  *Vous avez un site Internet?*
     **Vooz <u>ah</u>-vay uhn <u>seet</u> ihn-tair-<u>net</u>**

863.   Free Internet access.    *Accès Internet gratuit.*
       **Ax**-say ihn-tair-**net** grah-**twee**

864.   Free Wi-Fi.    *Le Wi-Fi gratuit.*    **Luh <u>wee</u>-fee grah-<u>twee</u>**

865.   I need to download a document.
       *Je dois télécharger un document.*
       **Zhuh dwah <u>tay</u>-lay-<u>shahr</u>-zhay uhn <u>doh</u>-cue-<u>mehn</u>**

866.   I need to print a document.    *Je dois imprimer un document.*
       **Zhuh dwahz <u>ihm</u>-pree-may uhn <u>doh</u>-cue-<u>mehn</u>**

867.   I need to download some software.
       *Je dois télécharger un logiciel.*
       **Zhuh dwah <u>tay</u>-lay-<u>shahr</u>-zhay uhn <u>loh</u>-zhee-<u>syel</u>**

868.   I need to save a file.    *Je dois sauvegarder un fichier.*
       **Zhuh dwah <u>sohv</u>-gar-day uhn <u>feesh</u>-yay**

869.   May I plug in my USB flash drive?
       *Je peux brancher ma clé USB?*
       **Zhuh puh <u>brehn</u>-shay mah <u>klay</u> oo-ess-<u>bay</u>**

870.   May I log on?    *Je peux ouvrir une session?*
       **Zhuh puh <u>oov</u>-reer oon <u>sess</u>-yion**

871.   I forgot my password.    *J'ai oublié mon mot de passe.*
       **Zhay <u>oob</u>-lee-<u>yay</u> mohn <u>moh</u> duh <u>pass</u>**

872.   May I send a fax?    *Je peux envoyer un fax?*
       **Zhuh puh <u>ehn</u>-vwah-<u>yay</u> uhn <u>fax</u>**

873.   I'd like to photocopy some documents.
       *Je voudrais photocopier des documents.*
       **Zhuh voo-<u>dray</u> pho-to-<u>cop</u>-yay day <u>doh</u>-cue-<u>mehn</u>**

# Chapter 8
## Idiomatic Expressions and Slang

## DESCRIBING PEOPLE

874. What a jerk! (m.)   *Quel con!*   **Kel <u>kohn</u>**

875. What an idiot!   *Quel idiot(e)!*   **Kel ee-<u>joe</u> / eed-<u>yut</u>**

876. He/She's a blockhead!   *C'est un(e) bourrique!*
**Set uhn / oon boo-<u>reek</u>**

877. They are real hippies!   *Ce sont des vrais babas.*
**Suh sohn day <u>vray</u> bah-<u>bah</u>**

878. He/She's a drunk.   *C'est un(e) ivrogne.*
**Set uhn/oon eev-<u>roh</u>-nyuh**

879. I think he/she's really drunk.
*Je crois qu'il est vraiment bourré.*
*Je crois qu'elle est vraiment bourrée.*
**Zhuh kwah <u>keel</u> ay <u>vray</u>-mehn <u>boo</u>-ray**
**Zhuh kwah <u>kell</u> ay <u>vray</u>-mehn <u>boo</u>-ray**

880. She's nice.   *Elle est sympa.*   **Ell ay <u>sihm</u>-pah**

881. He/She's really super-nice.   *Il/Elle est hyper sympa.*
**Eel/ell ay <u>ee</u>-pair <u>sihm</u>-pah**

882. They are such complainers!   *Ils sont tellement rouspéteurs!*
**Eel sohn <u>tell</u>-mehn <u>roos</u>-pay-<u>tuhr</u>**

883. It's cool.   *C'est cool.*   **Say <u>kool</u>**

884.  It's super cool.    *C'est hyper cool.*    **Say <u>ee</u>-pair kool**

885.  What a stupid movie!    *Quel film débile!*
      **<u>Kel</u> feem <u>day</u>-beel**

886.  Same difference. It's the same.    *C'est kif-kif.*    **Say <u>keef</u>-<u>keef</u>**

887.  This is so out of date/corny!    *C'est tellement ringard!*
      **Say <u>tell</u>-mehn <u>rihn</u>-gar**

888.  I'm broke!    *Je suis à sec!*    **Zhuh <u>sweez</u> ah <u>sek</u>**

889.  He/She is a cheapskate.    *Il/elle est radin(e).*
      **Eel <u>ay</u> rah-<u>dihn</u>    Ell <u>ay</u> rah-<u>deen</u>**

890.  My cousin is also so awkward.
      *Ma cousine est toujours tellement godiche.*
      **Mah koo-<u>zeen</u> ay too-<u>zhoor</u> <u>tell</u>-mehn go-<u>deesh</u>**

891.  Careful, he/she's very cunning!
      *Attention, il/elle est très roublard(e)!*
      **Att-en-<u>syion</u> eel/ell <u>ay</u> tray roob-<u>lar</u> / roob-<u>lard</u>**

892.  He/she's an odd-ball.    *Il/elle est déjanté(e).*
      **Eel / ell <u>ay</u> <u>day</u>-zhan-<u>tay</u>**

## FAMILY RELATIONSHIPS

---

893.  My pal.    *Mon pote.*    **Mohn <u>puht</u>**

894.  My brother.    *Mon frangin.*    **Mohn <u>frehn</u>-zhin**

895.  My sister.    *Ma frangine.*    **Ma <u>frehn</u>-zheen**

896.  My boyfriend    *Mon jules.*    **Mohn <u>zhool</u>**

897.  There's Uncle Bob!    *Voilà tonton Bob!*
      **Vwah-lah <u>tehn</u>-tehn <u>Bob</u>**

898.  Look, it's Aunt Carol!    *Regarde, c'est tata Carol!*
      **Ruh-<u>gard</u> say <u>tah</u>-ta <u>Ca</u>-rol**

899.  I have three kids.    *J'ai trois gosses/mômes.*
      **Zhay <u>twah</u> gahs/mome**

900.   I saw your kid (m.) yesterday.   *J'ai vu ton gamin hier.*
       **Zhay <u>voo</u> tohn gah-<u>mihn</u> ee-<u>air</u>**

## EMOTIONS

901.   She's in seventh heaven.   *Elle est aux anges.*
       **Ell ay <u>oze</u> ehnzh**

902.   He's pouting   *Il fait la tête.*   **Eel <u>fay</u> lah <u>tet</u>**

903.   He/she's crazy!   *Il/Elle est fou/folle!*   **Eel/Ell ay <u>foo</u>/<u>fuhl</u>**

904.   She's a little nuts!   *Elle est un peu zinzin!*
       **Ell <u>ay</u> uhn puh <u>zihn</u>-zihn**

905.   That man/woman is definitely insane!
       *Cet homme-là est vraiment cinglé!*
       *Cette femme-là est vraiment cinglée!*
       **Set <u>umm</u>-lah ay vray-<u>mehn</u> sihn-<u>glay</u>**
       **Set <u>fahm</u>-lah ay vray-<u>mehn</u> sihn-<u>glay</u>**

906.   I'm depressed.   *J'ai le cafard.*   **<u>Zhay</u> luh kah-<u>far</u>**

907.   I'm fed up!   *J'en ai marre!*   **<u>Zhehn</u> ay <u>mar</u>**

908.   She seems dazed.   *Elle a l'air vaseux.*   **Ell ah <u>lair</u> <u>vah</u>-suh**

909.   She's always scared.   *Elle a tout le temps la trouille.*
       **Ell ah <u>too</u> luh tehn lah <u>troo</u>-ee**

910.   It's normal to be scared before an exam.
       *C'est normal d'avoir le trac avant une épreuve.*
       **Say nor-<u>mahl</u> dahv-<u>wahr</u> luh <u>trahk</u> ahv-ehn oon <u>ay</u>-pruhv**

911.   I'm exhausted.   *Je suis crevé(e).*   **Zhuh swee <u>kruh</u>-vay**

912.   He's loosing his marbles.   *Il perd les pédales.*
       **Eel pair lay <u>ped</u>-ahl**

913.   I am so lazy!   *Je suis tellement flemmard(e)!*
       **Zhuh swee <u>tell</u>-mehn flehm-<u>ar</u> / flehm-<u>ard</u>**

914.   We are so lucky!   *On a de la veine!*   **Ohn <u>ah</u> duh lah <u>ven</u>**

## LOVE AND RELATIONSHIPS

915. He stood me up.     *Il m'a posé un lapin.*
Eel mah <u>poh</u>-zay uhn lah-<u>pihn</u>

916. She is fickle.     *Elle a un cœur d'artichaut.*
Ell ah uhn <u>kuhr</u> dar-tee-<u>shoh</u>

917. He's is only interested in passing love affairs.
*Il ne s'intéresse qu'aux amourettes.*
Eel nuh <u>sihn</u>-tair-ess <u>kohz</u> ah-moor-<u>et</u>

918. He's a real ladies' man.     *C'est un sacré dragueur.*
Set uhn sahk-<u>ray</u> dra-<u>guhr</u>

919. He's sweet-talking me.     *Il me fait du baratin.*
Eel <u>muh</u> fay doo <u>bah</u>-rah-<u>tihn</u>

920. I have a crush on her.     *J'ai le béguin pour elle.*
Zhay luh <u>bay</u>-ghin poor <u>ell</u>

921. He/she is hopelessly in love with me.
*Il est éperdument amoureux de moi.*
*Elle est éperdument amoureuse de moi.*
Eel ay <u>ay</u>-pair-doo-<u>mehn</u> ah-moor-<u>uh</u> duh <u>moi</u>
Ell ay <u>ay</u>-pair-doo-<u>mehn</u> ah-moor-<u>uhz</u> duh <u>moi</u>

922. It was love at first sight for them.
*C'était le coup de foudre entre eux.*
Say-tay luh <u>koo</u> duh <u>foo</u>-druh <u>ehntr</u> uh

923. He has a crush on his new neighbor.
*Il a flashé sur sa nouvelle voisine.*
Eel ah <u>flah</u>-shay soor sah <u>noo</u>-vell <u>vwah</u>-zeen

924. She's pretty enough to eat!     *Elle est belle à croquer!*
Ell ay <u>bell</u> ah <u>kroh</u>-kay

925. She has a crush on him.     *Elle craque pour lui.*
Ell <u>krak</u> poor <u>lwee</u>

926. He's going to dump me.     *Il va me larguer.*
Ee vah muh <u>lar</u>-gay

## COMMON ABBREVIATIONS

In the French language it is quite common to see abbreviated forms of longer words. These tend to be quite informal.

927. An addict. *Un accro.* **Uhn <u>ah</u>-kroh**

928. The afternoon. *Un aprem.* **Uhn <u>ahp</u>-rem**

929. An adolescent. *Un ado.* **Uhn <u>ah</u>-doh**

930. An apartment. *Un apart.* **Uhn <u>ah</u>-par**

931. A pre-dinner cocktail. *Un apéro.* **Uhn ah-<u>pay</u>-roh**

932. Catholic. *Catho.* **<u>Ka</u>-toh**

933. A college campus. *La fac.* **Lah <u>fak</u>**

934. Impeccable. *Impec.* **<u>Ihm</u>-pek**

935. A raincoat. *Un imper.* **Uhn <u>ihm</u>-pair**

936. McDonald's. *MacDo.* **<u>Mac</u>-doh**

937. A computer. *Un ordi.* **Uhn <u>ore</u>-dee**

938. Sensational. *Sensass.* **<u>Sen</u>-sass**

939. Working-class. *Prolo.* **<u>Proh</u>-loh**

## INTERJECTIONS

940. Great! *Génial!* **<u>Zhayn</u>-yahl**

941. Super! *Chouette/super!* **<u>Shoo</u>-wet / <u>soo</u>-pair**

942. Whatever! *Bof!* **Buhf**

943. I dare you! *Chiche!* **Sheesh**

944. Who cares? *Et après?* **Ay ah-pray**

945. I don't care! *Je m'en fiche!* **Zhuh <u>mohn</u> feesh**

946.  Darn!    *Mince!*    **Mihns**

947.  Oh, rats!    *La vache!*    **Lah** vahsh

948.  Whoopsie-daisy!    *Hop-là!*    **Up**-lah

949.  Damn!    *Merde!*    **Mare**-duh

950.  Yum, yum!    *Miam miam!*    **Myiam** myiam

951.  How stupid!    *C'est nul!*    **Say** nool

952.  What a dump!    *Quelle barraque!*    **kel bah-rak**

953.  Yuck!    *Berk!*    **Burk**

954.  What a mess!    *Quel bordel!*    **Kel bore-del**

955.  Mind your own business!    *Occupe-toi de tes oignons!*
**Oh-cyoop** twah duh **taze** uh-**nyion**

## SLANG

The following slang expressions are commonly used in informal conversation. The more standard French equivalent appears in brackets next to the sentences below where appropriate.

956.  We just bought a car. (une voiture)
*On vient d'acheter une bagnole.*
**Ohn vee-ehn dash-tay oon bahn-yuhl**

957.  I make a hundred big ones a day (les euros/dollars)
*Je gagne cent balles par jour.*
**Zuh gah-nyuh sehn bahl par zhoor**

958.  I hate the food here. (la nourriture)
*J'aime pas la bouffe ici.*    **Zhem pah lah boof ee-see**

959.  We really chowed down. (ate)    *On a bien bouffé.*
**Ohn ah byehn boo-fay**

960.  She just got a job! (un emploi)
*Elle vient de trouver un boulot!*
**Elle vyehn duh troo-vay uhn bool-loh**

961. Can you lend me this book? (un livre)
*Tu peux me prêter ce bouquin?*
**Too puh muh pret-tay suh boo-kihn**

962. Let's get out of here! (aller)    *On se casse!*    **Ohn suh kass**

963. She is chatting with her best friend. (parler)
*Elle cause avec sa meilleure amie.*
**Ell kohz ah-vek sah may-yer ah-mee**

964. How about going to the movies tonight? (le cinéma)
*Si on allait au cinoche ce soir?*
**See ohn ah-lay oh seen-ush suh swahr**

965. I love your new suit. (costume)
*J'aime bien ton nouveau costard.*
**Zhem byehn tohn noo-voh koh-star**

966. That's a crazy idea! (fou, m.; folle, f.)
*C'est une idée loufoque!*    **Set oon ee-day loo-fuhk**

967. We saw a funny movie last night. (comique)
*On a vu un film marrant hier soir.*
**Ohn ah voo uhn feem mah-rehn ee-yair swahr**

968. I love your new clothes. (vêtements)
*J'aime bien tes nouvelles fringues.*
**Zhem byehn tay noo-vel frihn-guh**

969. That guy is getting on my nerves. (homme)
*Ce type-là me tape sur les nerfs.*
**Suh teep-lah muh tahp soor lay nair**

970. He saw a guy that we all know. (homme)
*Il a vu un mec que nous connaissons tous.*
**Eel ah voo uhn mek kuh noo kuhn-ess-ohn toos**

971. What an ugly dress! (laid, m.; laide, f.)
*Quelle robe moche!*    **Kel ruhb mush**

972. They told us a really stupid story. (stupide)
*Ils nous ont raconté une histoire nunuche.*
**Ee nooz ohn rah-kohn-tay oon ees-twahr noo-noosh**

973. I don't understand! (comprendre)
*Je pige pas!*    <u>Zhuh</u> <u>peezh</u> pah

974. What is this thingamajig?    *C'est quoi, ce truc?*
**Say** <u>kwah</u> suh <u>trook</u>

975. What is this thingie for?    *Ça sert à quoi, ce bidule?*
**Sah** <u>sair</u> ah <u>kwah</u> suh bee-<u>dool</u>

976. Give me that whatchamacallit!    *Donne-moi cet engin!*
**Dun-**<u>mwah</u> set <u>ehn</u>-zhin

977. What's-his-name.    *Monsieur Untel.*    <u>Mohn</u>-syuh <u>uhn</u>-tel

978. What's-her-name.    *Madame Unetelle.*    <u>Mah</u>-dahm <u>oon</u>-tell

979. Whatever-his-name-is.    *Machin.*    <u>Ma</u>-shihn

980. Piece of cake!    *C'est du gâteau!*    **Say** <u>doo</u> gah-<u>toh</u>

981. I can't believe it!    *J'en reviens pas!*    **Zhehn** <u>ruh</u>-vyihn <u>pah</u>

982. I'll do that when pigs fly!
*Je ferai ça quand les poules auront les dents!*
*(lit. when hens have teeth)*
**Zhuh** <u>fuh</u>-ray sah kehn lay <u>pool</u> ohr-<u>ehn</u> lay <u>dehn</u>

983. It's a sure thing.    *C'est dans la poche.*    **Say** <u>dehn</u> lah <u>puhsh</u>

984. That's disgusting!    *C'est dégoutant!*    **Say** <u>day</u>-goo-tehn

985. I can't be in two places at once.
*Je ne peux pas être au four et au moulin.*
**Zhuh** nuh <u>puh</u> pahz <u>et</u>-ruh oh <u>foor</u> ay oh moo-<u>lihn</u>

986. It's not as bad as all that.    *Ce n'est pas la mer à boire.*
**Suh** nay <u>pah</u> lah <u>mare</u> ah <u>bwahr</u>

987. I have other fish to fry.    *J'ai d'autres chats à fouetter.*
**Zhay** <u>doht</u>-ruh <u>sha</u> ah <u>fweh</u>-tay

# PROVERBS

988. Where there's a will, there's a way.     *Vouloir c'est pouvoir.*
Vool-<u>wahr</u> say poov-<u>wahr</u>

989. To understand is to forgive.
*Tout comprendre, c'est tout pardonner.*
Too kom-<u>prehnd</u>-ruh say too par-dun-<u>ay</u>

990. Strike while the iron is hot.
*Battre le fer pendant qu'il est chaud.*
<u>Bah</u>-truh luh <u>fair</u> pehn-dehn keel ay <u>shoh</u>

991. Better late than never.     *Mieux vaut tard que jamais.*
Myuh voh <u>tar</u> kuh <u>zhah</u>-may

992. Clothes don't make the man.     *L'habit ne fait pas le moine.*
Lah-<u>bee</u> nuh fay <u>pah</u> luh <u>mwehn</u>-nuh

993. Rome wasn't built in a day.
*Rome ne s'est pas faite en un jour.*
<u>Rome</u> nuh say pah <u>fet</u> ehn uhn <u>zhoor</u>

994. There are other fish in the sea.
*Un de perdu, dix de retrouvés.*
Uhn duh pair-<u>doo</u> dees duh ruh-troo-<u>vay</u>

995. Practice makes perfect.
*C'est en forgeant qu'on devient forgeron.*
Say tuhn <u>for</u>-zhehn kohn duh-vyehn <u>forzh</u>-rohn

996. Every cloud has a silver lining.
*Après la pluie, le beau temps.*
Ah-pray lah <u>ploo</u>-ee luh boh <u>tehn</u>

997. No sooner said than done.     *Aussitôt dit, aussitôt fait.*
Oh-see-toh <u>dee</u> oh-see-toh <u>fay</u>

998. Desperate times call for desperate measures.
*Aux grands maux les grands remèdes.*
Oh grehn <u>moh</u> lay <u>grehn</u> ruh-<u>med</u>

999. Look before you leap.    *Il faut réfléchir avant d'agir.*
Eel foh <u>ray</u>-flay-sheer av-ehn <u>dah</u>-zheer

1000. Where there's smoke, there's fire.
*Il n'y a pas de fumée sans feu.*
Eel nyah pah duh foo-<u>may</u> sehn <u>fuh</u>

1001. When it rains, it pours.    *Un malheur ne vient jamais seul.*
Uhn mahl-<u>er</u> nuh vyehn <u>zha</u>-may <u>sull</u>

# Appendix
## More Useful Expressions

### Pronouns, Verbs, Number, Adjectives, Articles, and Negation

#### Pronouns

The following subject pronouns are useful to know:

Je (I)                          Nous (We)
Tu (You—informal)               Vous (You—formal and plural)
Il, Elle, On (He, She, One, We, It)   Ils, Elles (They—plural)

Sometimes you might hear French speakers using *on* rather than *nous* for "we."

#### Verbs

The following present-tense verb conjugations can be useful as a general reference.

##### Avoir: to have

| j' ai (I have) | nous avons (we have) |
|---|---|
| tu as (you have, informal) | vous avez (you have, formal and plural) |
| il/elle/on a  (he, she, one, it has) | ils/elles ont (they have, m and f) |

##### Être: to be

| je suis (I am) | nous sommes (we are) |
|---|---|
| tu es (you are, informal) | vous êtes (you are, formal and plural) |
| il/elle/on est (he, she, one, it is) | ils/elles sont (they are, m and f) |

**Faire:** to do, to make

| je fais ( I do) | nous faisons (we do) |
| --- | --- |
| tu fais (you do, informal) | vous faites (you do, formal and plural) |
| il/elle/on fait (he, she, one, it, does) | ils/elles font (they do, m and f) |

### Adjectives

French adjectives must agree with the noun that they are modifying in gender and number. Most adjectives have masculine and feminine forms, and singular and plural forms as well.

Il est méchant.    Ils sont méchants.
*He is mean.*    *They are mean. (m., pl.)*

Elle est méchante.    Elles sont méchantes.
*She is mean.*    *They are mean (f., pl.)*

Frequently, the feminine form is made by adding an "e." The plural form is usually made by adding an "s," unless it already ends in "s." Here are a few examples that follow this pattern:

| Masculine singular | Feminine singular | Masculine plural | Feminine plural |
| --- | --- | --- | --- |
| américain (American) | américaine | américains | américaines |
| anglais (English) | anglaise | anglais | anglaises |
| français (French) | française | français | françaises |
| froid (cold) | froide | froids | froides |
| grand (big) | grande | grands | grandes |
| intéressant (interesting) | intéressante | intéressants | intéressantes |
| mauvais (bad) | mauvaise | mauvais | mauvaises |
| patient (patient) | patiente | patients | patientes |
| petit (small) | petite | petits | petites |

Others follow a pattern of the masculine form ending in "-ieux," whereas the feminine form ends in "-ieuse." Note that the plural forms change as well:

| Masculine singular | Feminine singular | Masculine plural | Feminine plural |
|---|---|---|---|
| courageux (courageous) | courageuse | courageux | courageuses |
| ennuyeux (tired, bored) | ennuyeuse | ennuyeux | ennuyeuses |
| nerveux (nervous) | nerveuse | nerveux | nerveuses |
| sérieux (serious) | sérieuse | sérieux | sérieuses |
| studieux (studious) | studieuse | studieux | studieuses |

Some adjectives have irregular forms that must be memorized:

| Masculine singular | Feminine singular | Masculine plural | Feminine plural |
|---|---|---|---|
| beau (beautiful) | belle | beaux | belles |
| bon (good) | bonne | bons | bonnes |
| vieux (old) | vieille | vieux | vieilles |

Most adjectives follow the nouns they modify:

Je voudrais trouver un livre <u>intéressant</u>.
*I want to find an interesting book.*

Some adjectives, however, are placed before the nouns they modify. Students frequently use the acronym BANGS to remember them:

Beauty
On a trouvé une <u>belle</u> plage.
*We found a beautiful beach.*

Age
Posons notre question à ce <u>jeune</u> homme.
*Let's ask this young man our question.*

Newness
J'ai un <u>nouveau</u> passeport.
*I have a new passport.*

Goodness
On aimerait déjeuner dans un <u>bon</u> café au centre-ville.
*We'd like to have lunch in a good café downtown.*

Size
Il y a un <u>petit</u> problème avec notre chambre.
*There's a small problem with our room.*

## Articles

As mentioned at the beginning of *1001 Easy French Phrses,* every French noun is either masculine or feminine. When you learn a new word, try to learn the article with it.

The definite articles, which translate as "the" in English, are as follows:

| | |
|---|---|
| le (masculine, singular) | Attention—Le chien est très méchant!<br>*Watch out—the dog is quite mean!* |
| la (feminine, singular) | La compagnie de vol est très respectée.<br>*The airline is quite respected.* |
| l' (m and f in front of a vowel) | Donnez-moi l'addition, s'il vous plaît.<br>*Give me the check, please.* |
| les (plural, both) | Les magazines coûtent très cher ici.<br>*Magazines are quite expensive here.* |

## Negation

You will notice that the typical verbal construction follows the S (subject) V (verb) O (object) form.

| Je | <u>vois</u> | <u>l'hôtel</u>. |
|---|---|---|
| I | see | the hotel. |
| S | V | O |

In order to make the sentence negative, just place "ne . . . pas" around the verb:

| Je | ne | vois | pas | l'hôtel. |
|---|---|---|---|---|
| I | don't | see | | the hotel. |

# More Learning Resources

Check out these additional French resources:

*General French culture:*

Cultural Services of the French Embassy
http://www.frenchculture.org/

French.about.com
http://french.about.com/

*General French-language learning:*

BBC
http://www.bbc.co.uk/languages/french/

Bonjour.com
http://www.bonjour.com/

French Language Learning Library
http://www.languagelearninglibrary.org/french/

TV5 Monde
http://www.tv5.org/TV5Site/enseigner-apprendre-francais/accueil_
   apprendre.php

*French vocabulary:*

Lingolex
http://www.lingolex.com/french.htm

*On-line dictionary:*

Word Reference.com
http://www.wordreference.com/

French-linguistics
http://www.french-linguistics.co.uk/dictionary/

*French grammar:*

Tex's French grammar
http://www.laits.utexas.edu/tex/

Languageguide.org
http://www.languageguide.org/francais/grammar/

UVA grammar practice website
http://faculty.virginia.edu/ajmlevine/grammar/a_grammarindex.html

*Pronunciation:*

Essortment.com
http://www.essortment.com/all/frenchpronunc_rsih.htm

French.about.com
http://french.about.com/od/pronunciation/French_Pronunciation
    _Lessons_and_Activities.htm

*Etiquette:*

Kwintessential
http://www.kwintessential.co.uk/resources/global-etiquette/france
    -country-profile.html

# Acknowledgments

I would like to thank those who have assisted me with this project, directly and indirectly. I gratefully acknowledge Rochelle Kronzek and Janet Kopito, editors at Dover Publications, Inc., for the opportunity to create a book helping French-language learners; Sandrine Siméon, for proofreading the phrases and making them as Frenchified as possible; Meredith Doran, for friendship and fulfilling dialogue about language learning and teaching; Bénédicte Monicat, for being a kind and encouraging colleague; the students at Penn State University, who continue to teach me so much; Barbara Campbell Hall, for her friendship and sly wit; my Tweeps, for keeping this Minnesotan's English as standard as possible; and my parents, Bob and Margaret McCoy, whose deep commitment to their own personal interests has always inspired me.

# Index

# A CATALOG OF SELECTED
## DOVER BOOKS
### IN ALL FIELDS OF INTEREST

# A CATALOG OF SELECTED DOVER BOOKS IN ALL FIELDS OF INTEREST

100 BEST-LOVED POEMS, Edited by Philip Smith. "The Passionate Shepherd to His Love," "Shall I compare thee to a summer's day?" "Death, be not proud," "The Raven," "The Road Not Taken," plus works by Blake, Wordsworth, Byron, Shelley, Keats, many others. 96pp. 5 3/16 x 8¼. 0-486-28553-7

100 SMALL HOUSES OF THE THIRTIES, Brown-Blodgett Company. Exterior photographs and floor plans for 100 charming structures. Illustrations of models accompanied by descriptions of interiors, color schemes, closet space, and other amenities. 200 illustrations. 112pp. 8⅜ x 11. 0-486-44131-8

1000 TURN-OF-THE-CENTURY HOUSES: With Illustrations and Floor Plans, Herbert C. Chivers. Reproduced from a rare edition, this showcase of homes ranges from cottages and bungalows to sprawling mansions. Each house is meticulously illustrated and accompanied by complete floor plans. 256pp. 9⅜ x 12¼. 0-486-45596-3

101 GREAT AMERICAN POEMS, Edited by The American Poetry & Literacy Project. Rich treasury of verse from the 19th and 20th centuries includes works by Edgar Allan Poe, Robert Frost, Walt Whitman, Langston Hughes, Emily Dickinson, T. S. Eliot, other notables. 96pp. 5 3/16 x 8¼. 0-486-40158-8

101 GREAT SAMURAI PRINTS, Utagawa Kuniyoshi. Kuniyoshi was a master of the warrior woodblock print — and these 18th-century illustrations represent the pinnacle of his craft. Full-color portraits of renowned Japanese samurais pulse with movement, passion, and remarkably fine detail. 112pp. 8⅜ x 11. 0-486-46523-3

ABC OF BALLET, Janet Grosser. Clearly worded, abundantly illustrated little guide defines basic ballet-related terms: arabesque, battement, pas de chat, relevé, sissonne, many others. Pronunciation guide included. Excellent primer. 48pp. 4 3/16 x 5¾. 0-486-40871-X

ACCESSORIES OF DRESS: An Illustrated Encyclopedia, Katherine Lester and Bess Viola Oerke. Illustrations of hats, veils, wigs, cravats, shawls, shoes, gloves, and other accessories enhance an engaging commentary that reveals the humor and charm of the many-sided story of accessorized apparel. 644 figures and 59 plates. 608pp. 6 ⅛ x 9¼. 0-486-43378-1

ADVENTURES OF HUCKLEBERRY FINN, Mark Twain. Join Huck and Jim as their boyhood adventures along the Mississippi River lead them into a world of excitement, danger, and self-discovery. Humorous narrative, lyrical descriptions of the Mississippi valley, and memorable characters. 224pp. 5 3/16 x 8¼. 0-486-28061-6

ALICE STARMORE'S BOOK OF FAIR ISLE KNITTING, Alice Starmore. A noted designer from the region of Scotland's Fair Isle explores the history and techniques of this distinctive, stranded-color knitting style and provides copious illustrated instructions for 14 original knitwear designs. 208pp. 8⅜ x 10⅞. 0-486-47218-3

**Browse over 9,000 books at www.doverpublications.com**

# CATALOG OF DOVER BOOKS

ALICE'S ADVENTURES IN WONDERLAND, Lewis Carroll. Beloved classic about a little girl lost in a topsy-turvy land and her encounters with the White Rabbit, March Hare, Mad Hatter, Cheshire Cat, and other delightfully improbable characters. 42 illustrations by Sir John Tenniel. 96pp. 5³⁄₁₆ x 8¼.　　　　　　　　0-486-27543-4

AMERICA'S LIGHTHOUSES: An Illustrated History, Francis Ross Holland. Profusely illustrated fact-filled survey of American lighthouses since 1716. Over 200 stations — East, Gulf, and West coasts, Great Lakes, Hawaii, Alaska, Puerto Rico, the Virgin Islands, and the Mississippi and St. Lawrence Rivers. 240pp. 8 x 10¾.
　　　　　　　　　　　　　　　　　　　　　　　　　　0-486-25576-X

AN ENCYCLOPEDIA OF THE VIOLIN, Alberto Bachmann. Translated by Frederick H. Martens. Introduction by Eugene Ysaye. First published in 1925, this renowned reference remains unsurpassed as a source of essential information, from construction and evolution to repertoire and technique. Includes a glossary and 73 illustrations. 496pp. 6⅛ x 9¼.　　　　　　　　　　　　　　　0-486-46618-3

ANIMALS: 1,419 Copyright-Free Illustrations of Mammals, Birds, Fish, Insects, etc., Selected by Jim Harter. Selected for its visual impact and ease of use, this outstanding collection of wood engravings presents over 1,000 species of animals in extremely lifelike poses. Includes mammals, birds, reptiles, amphibians, fish, insects, and other invertebrates. 284pp. 9 x 12.　　　　　　　　　　　　0-486-23766-4

THE ANNALS, Tacitus. Translated by Alfred John Church and William Jackson Brodribb. This vital chronicle of Imperial Rome, written by the era's great historian, spans A.D. 14-68 and paints incisive psychological portraits of major figures, from Tiberius to Nero. 416pp. 5³⁄₁₆ x 8¼.　　　　　　　　　0-486-45236-0

ANTIGONE, Sophocles. Filled with passionate speeches and sensitive probing of moral and philosophical issues, this powerful and often-performed Greek drama reveals the grim fate that befalls the children of Oedipus. Footnotes. 64pp. 5³⁄₁₆ x 8 ¼.　　　　　　　　　　　　　　　　　　0-486-27804-2

ART DECO DECORATIVE PATTERNS IN FULL COLOR, Christian Stoll. Reprinted from a rare 1910 portfolio, 160 sensuous and exotic images depict a breathtaking array of florals, geometrics, and abstracts — all elegant in their stark simplicity. 64pp. 8⅜ x 11.　　　　　　　　　　　　　　　　　0-486-44862-2

THE ARTHUR RACKHAM TREASURY: 86 Full-Color Illustrations, Arthur Rackham. Selected and Edited by Jeff A. Menges. A stunning treasury of 86 full-page plates span the famed English artist's career, from *Rip Van Winkle* (1905) to masterworks such as *Undine, A Midsummer Night's Dream,* and *Wind in the Willows* (1939). 96pp. 8⅜ x 11.
　　　　　　　　　　　　　　　　　　　　　　　　　　0-486-44685-9

THE AUTHENTIC GILBERT & SULLIVAN SONGBOOK, W. S. Gilbert and A. S. Sullivan. The most comprehensive collection available, this songbook includes selections from every one of Gilbert and Sullivan's light operas. Ninety-two numbers are presented uncut and unedited, and in their original keys. 410pp. 9 x 12.
　　　　　　　　　　　　　　　　　　　　　　　　　　0-486-23482-7

THE AWAKENING, Kate Chopin. First published in 1899, this controversial novel of a New Orleans wife's search for love outside a stifling marriage shocked readers. Today, it remains a first-rate narrative with superb characterization. New introductory Note. 128pp. 5³⁄₁₆ x 8¼.　　　　　　　　　　0-486-27786-0

BASIC DRAWING, Louis Priscilla. Beginning with perspective, this commonsense manual progresses to the figure in movement, light and shade, anatomy, drapery, composition, trees and landscape, and outdoor sketching. Black-and-white illustrations throughout. 128pp. 8⅜ x 11.　　　　　　　　0-486-45815-6

**Browse over 9,000 books at www.doverpublications.com**

THE BATTLES THAT CHANGED HISTORY, Fletcher Pratt. Historian profiles 16 crucial conflicts, ancient to modern, that changed the course of Western civilization. Gripping accounts of battles led by Alexander the Great, Joan of Arc, Ulysses S. Grant, other commanders. 27 maps. 352pp. 5⅜ x 8½. 0-486-41129-X

BEETHOVEN'S LETTERS, Ludwig van Beethoven. Edited by Dr. A. C. Kalischer. Features 457 letters to fellow musicians, friends, greats, patrons, and literary men. Reveals musical thoughts, quirks of personality, insights, and daily events. Includes 15 plates. 410pp. 5⅜ x 8½. 0-486-22769-3

BERNICE BOBS HER HAIR AND OTHER STORIES, F. Scott Fitzgerald. This brilliant anthology includes 6 of Fitzgerald's most popular stories: "The Diamond as Big as the Ritz," the title tale, "The Offshore Pirate," "The Ice Palace," "The Jelly Bean," and "May Day." 176pp. 5⅜ x 8½. 0-486-47049-0

BESLER'S BOOK OF FLOWERS AND PLANTS: 73 Full-Color Plates from Hortus Eystettensis, 1613, Basilius Besler. Here is a selection of magnificent plates from the Hortus Eystettensis, which vividly illustrated and identified the plants, flowers, and trees that thrived in the legendary German garden at Eichstätt. 80pp. 8⅜ x 11. 0-486-46005-3

THE BOOK OF KELLS, Edited by Blanche Cirker. Painstakingly reproduced from a rare facsimile edition, this volume contains full-page decorations, portraits, illustrations, plus a sampling of textual leaves with exquisite calligraphy and ornamentation. 32 full-color illustrations. 32pp. 9⅜ x 12¼. 0-486-24345-1

THE BOOK OF THE CROSSBOW: With an Additional Section on Catapults and Other Siege Engines, Ralph Payne-Gallwey. Fascinating study traces history and use of crossbow as military and sporting weapon, from Middle Ages to modern times. Also covers related weapons: balistas, catapults, Turkish bows, more. Over 240 illustrations. 400pp. 7¼ x 10⅛. 0-486-28720-3

THE BUNGALOW BOOK: Floor Plans and Photos of 112 Houses, 1910, Henry L. Wilson. Here are 112 of the most popular and economic blueprints of the early 20th century — plus an illustration or photograph of each completed house. A wonderful time capsule that still offers a wealth of valuable insights. 160pp. 8⅜ x 11. 0-486-45104-6

THE CALL OF THE WILD, Jack London. A classic novel of adventure, drawn from London's own experiences as a Klondike adventurer, relating the story of a heroic dog caught in the brutal life of the Alaska Gold Rush. Note. 64pp. 5³⁄₁₆ x 8¼. 0-486-26472-6

CANDIDE, Voltaire. Edited by Francois-Marie Arouet. One of the world's great satires since its first publication in 1759. Witty, caustic skewering of romance, science, philosophy, religion, government — nearly all human ideals and institutions. 112pp. 5³⁄₁₆ x 8¼. 0-486-26689-3

CELEBRATED IN THEIR TIME: Photographic Portraits from the George Grantham Bain Collection, Edited by Amy Pastan. With an Introduction by Michael Carlebach. Remarkable portrait gallery features 112 rare images of Albert Einstein, Charlie Chaplin, the Wright Brothers, Henry Ford, and other luminaries from the worlds of politics, art, entertainment, and industry. 128pp. 8⅜ x 11. 0-486-46754-6

CHARIOTS FOR APOLLO: The NASA History of Manned Lunar Spacecraft to 1969, Courtney G. Brooks, James M. Grimwood, and Loyd S. Swenson, Jr. This illustrated history by a trio of experts is the definitive reference on the Apollo spacecraft and lunar modules. It traces the vehicles' design, development, and operation in space. More than 100 photographs and illustrations. 576pp. 6¾ x 9¼. 0-486-46756-2

A CHRISTMAS CAROL, Charles Dickens. This engrossing tale relates Ebenezer Scrooge's ghostly journeys through Christmases past, present, and future and his ultimate transformation from a harsh and grasping old miser to a charitable and compassionate human being. 80pp. 5³⁄₁₆ x 8¼. 0-486-26865-9

COMMON SENSE, Thomas Paine. First published in January of 1776, this highly influential landmark document clearly and persuasively argued for American separation from Great Britain and paved the way for the Declaration of Independence. 64pp. 5³⁄₁₆ x 8¼. 0-486-29602-4

THE COMPLETE SHORT STORIES OF OSCAR WILDE, Oscar Wilde. Complete texts of "The Happy Prince and Other Tales," "A House of Pomegranates," "Lord Arthur Savile's Crime and Other Stories," "Poems in Prose," and "The Portrait of Mr. W. H." 208pp. 5³⁄₁₆ x 8¼. 0-486-45216-6

COMPLETE SONNETS, William Shakespeare. Over 150 exquisite poems deal with love, friendship, the tyranny of time, beauty's evanescence, death, and other themes in language of remarkable power, precision, and beauty. Glossary of archaic terms. 80pp. 5³⁄₁₆ x 8¼. 0-486-26686-9

THE COUNT OF MONTE CRISTO: Abridged Edition, Alexandre Dumas. Falsely accused of treason, Edmond Dantès is imprisoned in the bleak Chateau d'If. After a hair-raising escape, he launches an elaborate plot to extract a bitter revenge against those who betrayed him. 448pp. 5³⁄₁₆ x 8¼. 0-486-45643-9

CRAFTSMAN BUNGALOWS: Designs from the Pacific Northwest, Yoho & Merritt. This reprint of a rare catalog, showcasing the charming simplicity and cozy style of Craftsman bungalows, is filled with photos of completed homes, plus floor plans and estimated costs. An indispensable resource for architects, historians, and illustrators. 112pp. 10 x 7. 0-486-46875-5

CRAFTSMAN BUNGALOWS: 59 Homes from "The Craftsman," Edited by Gustav Stickley. Best and most attractive designs from Arts and Crafts Movement publication — 1903–1916 — includes sketches, photographs of homes, floor plans, descriptive text. 128pp. 8¼ x 11. 0-486-25829-7

CRIME AND PUNISHMENT, Fyodor Dostoyevsky. Translated by Constance Garnett. Supreme masterpiece tells the story of Raskolnikov, a student tormented by his own thoughts after he murders an old woman. Overwhelmed by guilt and terror, he confesses and goes to prison. 480pp. 5³⁄₁₆ x 8¼. 0-486-41587-2

THE DECLARATION OF INDEPENDENCE AND OTHER GREAT DOCUMENTS OF AMERICAN HISTORY: 1775-1865, Edited by John Grafton. Thirteen compelling and influential documents: Henry's "Give Me Liberty or Give Me Death," Declaration of Independence, The Constitution, Washington's First Inaugural Address, The Monroe Doctrine, The Emancipation Proclamation, Gettysburg Address, more. 64pp. 5³⁄₁₆ x 8¼. 0-486-41124-9

THE DESERT AND THE SOWN: Travels in Palestine and Syria, Gertrude Bell. "The female Lawrence of Arabia," Gertrude Bell wrote captivating, perceptive accounts of her travels in the Middle East. This intriguing narrative, accompanied by 160 photos, traces her 1905 sojourn in Lebanon, Syria, and Palestine. 368pp. 5⅜ x 8½. 0-486-46876-3

A DOLL'S HOUSE, Henrik Ibsen. Ibsen's best-known play displays his genius for realistic prose drama. An expression of women's rights, the play climaxes when the central character, Nora, rejects a smothering marriage and life in "a doll's house." 80pp. 5³⁄₁₆ x 8¼. 0-486-27062-9

**DOOMED SHIPS: Great Ocean Liner Disasters**, William H. Miller, Jr. Nearly 200 photographs, many from private collections, highlight tales of some of the vessels whose pleasure cruises ended in catastrophe: the *Morro Castle, Normandie, Andrea Doria, Europa*, and many others. 128pp. 8⅞ x 11¾. 0-486-45366-9

**THE DORÉ BIBLE ILLUSTRATIONS**, Gustave Doré. Detailed plates from the Bible: the Creation scenes, Adam and Eve, horrifying visions of the Flood, the battle sequences with their monumental crowds, depictions of the life of Jesus, 241 plates in all. 241pp. 9 x 12. 0-486-23004-X

**DRAWING DRAPERY FROM HEAD TO TOE**, Cliff Young. Expert guidance on how to draw shirts, pants, skirts, gloves, hats, and coats on the human figure, including folds in relation to the body, pull and crush, action folds, creases, more. Over 200 drawings. 48pp. 8¼ x 11. 0-486-45591-2

**DUBLINERS**, James Joyce. A fine and accessible introduction to the work of one of the 20th century's most influential writers, this collection features 15 tales, including a masterpiece of the short-story genre, "The Dead." 160pp. 5³⁄₁₆ x 8¼.

0-486-26870-5

**EASY-TO-MAKE POP-UPS**, Joan Irvine. Illustrated by Barbara Reid. Dozens of wonderful ideas for three-dimensional paper fun — from holiday greeting cards with moving parts to a pop-up menagerie. Easy-to-follow, illustrated instructions for more than 30 projects. 299 black-and-white illustrations. 96pp. 8⅜ x 11.

0-486-44622-0

**EASY-TO-MAKE STORYBOOK DOLLS: A "Novel" Approach to Cloth Dollmaking**, Sherralyn St. Clair. Favorite fictional characters come alive in this unique beginner's dollmaking guide. Includes patterns for Pollyanna, Dorothy from *The Wonderful Wizard of Oz*, Mary of *The Secret Garden*, plus easy-to-follow instructions, 263 black-and-white illustrations, and an 8-page color insert. 112pp. 8¼ x 11. 0-486-47360-0

**EINSTEIN'S ESSAYS IN SCIENCE**, Albert Einstein. Speeches and essays in accessible, everyday language profile influential physicists such as Niels Bohr and Isaac Newton. They also explore areas of physics to which the author made major contributions. 128pp. 5 x 8. 0-486-47011-3

**EL DORADO: Further Adventures of the Scarlet Pimpernel**, Baroness Orczy. A popular sequel to *The Scarlet Pimpernel*, this suspenseful story recounts the Pimpernel's attempts to rescue the Dauphin from imprisonment during the French Revolution. An irresistible blend of intrigue, period detail, and vibrant characterizations. 352pp. 5³⁄₁₆ x 8¼. 0-486-44026-5

**ELEGANT SMALL HOMES OF THE TWENTIES: 99 Designs from a Competition**, Chicago Tribune. Nearly 100 designs for five- and six-room houses feature New England and Southern colonials, Normandy cottages, stately Italianate dwellings, and other fascinating snapshots of American domestic architecture of the 1920s. 112pp. 9 x 12. 0-486-46910-7

**THE ELEMENTS OF STYLE: The Original Edition**, William Strunk, Jr. This is the book that generations of writers have relied upon for timeless advice on grammar, diction, syntax, and other essentials. In concise terms, it identifies the principal requirements of proper style and common errors. 64pp. 5⅜ x 8½. 0-486-44798-7

**THE ELUSIVE PIMPERNEL**, Baroness Orczy. Robespierre's revolutionaries find their wicked schemes thwarted by the heroic Pimpernel — Sir Percival Blakeney. In this thrilling sequel, Chauvelin devises a plot to eliminate the Pimpernel and his wife. 272pp. 5³⁄₁₆ x 8¼. 0-486-45464-9

**Browse over 9,000 books at www.doverpublications.com**